THE MORAL MEASURE OF LITERATURE

Also by Keith F. McKean

CROSS CURRENTS IN THE SOUTH

THE MORAL MEASURE

OF LITERATURE

by

Keith F. McKean

ALAN SWALLOW
DENVER

FOREWORD

I began this work in graduate school at the University of Michigan, and had the help of many good friends there. I think especially of Professors Joe Lee Davis, Norman E. Nelson, Louis I. Bredvold, and Warner G. Rice; and then, too, of Austin Warren, who "christened" an early draft of this document and an early addition to my family on the same spring day.

I am grateful also to the North Carolina State College Research and Development Committee. Their generous support has made it possible for me to continue my work and to publish this volume.

The problem of the moral measure of literature raises an endlessly interesting complex of issues, and some of them are touched on in this study. What follows has been a useful point of departure for me, and I hope it will be for others.

KEITH F. McKEAN

Raleigh, North Carolina
September 1, 1960

Contents

CHAPTER I

The Problem

It is often said that this is an age of literary criticism, and indeed, the number of first rate minds who have spent their energy on the art in the last fifty years is impressive.

Still, not everyone agrees. Karl Shapiro, for one, suggests sourly that the "new criticism" is bad for poetry. And "suggests" is hardly the word for what Shapiro says. Rather, he shouts, full volume, page after page, that contemporary critics are killing poetry. He warns the young artist against the entire tribe, and especially cautions them to beware of Ezra Pound and T. S. Eliot. In fact, if Shapiro discovers that a young writer is already acquainted with either one of these gentlemen, he gives up on the fledging. The deadly infection is already too deep.

But anyone who indiscriminately warns young writers against the new critics does American letters a disservice. The truth is that many of the critics, instead of being hostile to poetry, are themselves leading poets. The names of William Empson, Yvor Winters, T. S. Eliot, Allen Tate, John Crowe Ransom, Mark Van Doren, R. P. Blackmur, Ezra Pound, Randall Jarrell, and Shapiro himself, all remind us that not even Solomon could separate the critics from the creative artists, because the best performer in both fields is often the same person. In addition, many of the critics are teachers of literature as well as poets, and their criticism embodies their theories of composition as

9

well as their literary values. Any writer can learn from them, and the violent differences among the critics clearly indicates that there is no dull sameness about their ideas which might discourage new talent.

The new critics, then, are those who care the most for letters. They have devoted their lives to literature; and their critical writing, no less than all the rest, is a significant part of their contribution to our literature, for criticism is itself an art.

Shapiro's blast at criticism certainly livens things up a bit, but his blunt attack is not really helpful. For one thing, personal pique seems to motivate this angry protestant. And anyone who publishes a big, fat volume of criticism which damns the art, and completely dead-pan, too, is at least guilty of having very little sense of humor. If one must bring out such a book, then I suppose the title of this volume is appropriate and even descriptive, for it is called *In Defense of Ignorance*. If nothing else, Shapiro is skilled in the art of self defense.

While literary criticsm, old or new, will probably not suffer seriously from Shapiro's intemperate attack, still it is endangered by another suspicious attitude which is more common, more moderate and which seems to be more plausible. I refer to those critics of criticism who try to limit the critic's range by insisting that certain principles and standards are simply irrelevant to the value of the work. They may argue, for instance, that psychology, economics, or ethics should be strictly "off limits."

One of these attempts to limit the critic's scope is particularly important for this study, because it is the relatively new idea that the critic should not mix ethics with art. The quarrel here is usually about the critic's function, for many who hold the view would agree that the censor or the minister may measure literature by moral standards, but they believe that

10

the professional critic should keep his hands off, because they feel that the morality of the art is really irrelevant to its worth. The persons who are inclined to take this view may range all the way from the "scientific" scholar to the basement beatnik and just about the only thing they can agree on is the proposition that one should consider the work separate from its causes and its effects. They all try to understand or evaluate the work with what they feel is uniquely appropriate to the art. And ethical principles, they will agree, are somehow inappropriate.

This particular effort to separate literary art from ethics is one which most seriously limits the critic's effectiveness, for what most distinguishes literature from the other arts, what is, in truth, unique about the art, is its moral quality. It may be that moral standards are inappropriate to other arts, music, for instance, but they seem to be as relevant to literature as they are to life itself. Living necessarily involves values. One can not move a muscle without implying that it is desirable to do so. And of all the arts literature is the one that most persuades us of the qualities of actual experience, with its symbolic and dramatic representation of ideas, action and emotion. Literature is important to us precisely because of the values we find there.

If the subject matter of literary art is the full range of human values, then ethical principles are always relevant; and the more serious the work, the more useful they may be in understanding and judging it. In brief, I would say that moral standards provide us with indispensable tests of literary excellence.

It is not possible, moreover, to separate sharply the aesthetic aspects of a work from the other features, because everything in the art is there because of the artist's choice. Everything in the work is a part of the aesthetic whole. Literary reality, then,

11

is a carefully framed and controlled kind of actuality, with every element displaying the artist's own beliefs, his own values. His choice of subject and his treatment of it are evidence of his attitudes. As Irwin Edman points out in *The World, the Arts and the Artist,* the artist is "a commentator on life and in his immediate and imaginative way a philosopher." Thus, literature not only represents life, it evaluates it.

And literary art exhibits the writer's values both explicitly and implicitly. In the lyric poem, the sermon, or essay, we have an explicit expression of ideas and attitudes. The device of the intruding author also allows a writer to enter directly into the piece to speak his mind. But in addition to these obvious and open ways in which the author reveals his own values, there are more subtle ways of accomplishing the same end. His management of the action, for instance, may serve to judge what goes on in his work; or a careful choice of evaluative language may reveal his feelings. As Gustav Mueller suggests in *The World as Spectacle,* even the form of a work may embody "the feeling for what is important."

If literature itself is an evaluation of experience, both explicitly and by implication, then any adequate judgment of the art must measure the evaluation by the critic's own moral standards. And especially so because literature is addressed to the public and necessarily tries to persuade the audience to attend to its own point of view. In this sense you can say that the work leads a life of its own, independent of the author and anything he may have intended. It influences people in one way or another, and no work, good or bad, is rhetorically neutral. In *Science and Criticism* Herbert Muller argues this point when he observes:

> Like it or not, literature has, in fact, always been a "power of conduct." It has schooled purpose and desire, inculcated values and ideals, which is to say the ideas that men can

12

sing about. . . . One may say that the writer should not
deliberately aim to instruct or edify: literature should
not begin as a criticism of life. But it cannot help ending
so.[1]

And James Farrell in *A Note On Literary Criticism* high-
lights the important social role that literature can play when
he points out:

> In providing content, then, art serves an objective function
> in society. It presents material for the judgment of life
> and its phenomena; and along with this material it offers
> judgments on the material. It makes the reader more
> intensely conscious of the problems of life, of the pre-
> dicaments of people, the possibilities and the limitations
> in living, the diversities in human experience, and some
> of the meanings, potential and actual, in this human
> experience. It makes value judgments on conditions,
> actions, thoughts, situations, environments, hopes, despairs,
> ideals, dreams, and fantasies. It provides its audience
> with additional equipment in proceeding with their own
> lives, and in the outward extension of their interests. It
> points their emotions, their impulses, their wishes, and
> their thoughts toward or away from certain goals. It
> creates, in an ideal and formal sense, the consciousness
> of an epoch, and is thus one of the instruments that work
> toward moulding and remoulding the human conscious-
> ness.[2]

The argument for the moral measure of literature, therefore, rests primarily on the belief that literature mirrors all
kinds of experience, evaluates it, and persuades. And we have
agreed that someone in the society will probably take account
of the moral quality of literature; the only practical question
is whether the professional critic should consider it a significant
part of his function.

My aim in this study is to analyze and evaluate the theory
and the practice of three American critics who *do* consider the

13

moral measure of literature to be primary. They are Irving Babbitt, Paul Elmer More, and Yvor Winters.

Why these three? There are really two reasons why I focus on this particular trio, and one of them is personal. I am sympathetic to their particular approach. I came on these men in my own search for a way of accounting for the moral value of a work, and I was attracted to all three by their desire to treat literature as a part of the general life, their strong conviction that literature is important because it can serve as a guide to the good life.

Beyond this rather private reason for centering on Babbitt, More, and Winters, however, there is a more public one. These three critics all raise an important point in the history of American criticism. Babbitt and More, for instance, are not "new" critics in style or technique, yet they overlap some of the new critics in time and they share several of their points of view. Yvor Winters particularly is often said to be some sort of Neo-Humanist and there is, as we shall see, some reason to link him with the earlier men, but in many significant ways Winters is entirely his own man and quite clearly independent of the others. In fact, I hope to show that Winters is free of the worst faults of both Babbitt and More and yet he retains some of their virtues. In addition, Winters makes several contributions to criticism that are quite different from anything we find in the fathers of Neo-Humanism. By centering on these three critics, I may inadvertently reinforce a common illusion that they are closely related, but my ambition is to show that a careful examination of their work reveals how each one differs from the other two.

I hope it is clear, also, that my sympathy for the idea of the moral measure of literature is balanced by the realization that there are in practice at least two serious pitfalls in this approach. One is the possibility that the ethical critic may treat the art

14

as if it were only a moral thesis. Any poem, for instance, can be dealt with as if it were a prose statement, but that is only one aspect of the art. While it may be too much to ask that one approach account for the whole, still the moral critic who deals only with the paraphrasable content of a poem is much more limited than he need be.

A second hazard in the moral approach is that the critic may be attracted away from the art itself by his interest in the ethical implications of the work. It is not hard to see why this might happen. The ethical critic is quite sensitive to the right and wrong of conduct, and the danger is that he may turn his attention away from the art altogether to dwell on the more general social problem.

These two difficulties, then, are apt to plague the moral critic and the best of them will somehow avoid the excess. Before we come directly to the work of our first critic, Irving Babbitt, it may be useful to see how some of the key figures in the history of Western criticism have faced up to these and other problems related to the moral measure of literature.

CHAPTER II

Some Solutions of the Problem

Criticism is as old as literary art and we can set the stage for our study of three moderns if we see how certain critics in the past have dealt with the ethical aspects of literature. I have chosen five contrasting pairs, ten men in all, and they are arranged in roughly chronological order. Such a list must naturally be selective, and the treatment of each man is brief, for I am interested only in their general ideas on the moral measure of literature. Altogether, the list will give us considerable variety in attitudes and some typical ones, for these critics range all the way from censors to those who consider art above ethics, all the way from Plato to Poe. And most of the great periods are represented, because we will compare Plato and Aristotle from the golden age of Greece; Stephen Gosson and Sir Philip Sidney from renaissance England; Dr. Johnson and William Hazlitt of the eighteenth and early nineteenth centuries in England; and James Russell Lowell and Edgar Allan Poe of nineteenth century American letters.

Plato and Aristotle

Plato and Aristotle agree on some vital literary issues. They both measure literature by moral standards, and in their political writings both allow for censorship, but the differences between them are also significant. While Aristotle censors literature only for the young, Plato would banish all poets from his ideal state. Even more important, in his *Poetics,* Aristotle differs somewhat from Plato when he moves in the direction of treating literature as a unique thing, separate and apart from its causes and its effects.

All through *The Republic,* Plato attends to the way art relates to the general life and ultimately to a good life for his citizens. In short, he is constantly concerned with the ethical effects. When he discusses the subject matter of poetry, he asks what moral effect the scenes will have. When he turns briefly to literary style, in the Third Book, he again looks to the effect on the audience. He explains that his citizens must not be corrupted by any of the misrepresentations of the gods or heroes that one finds in much poetry, and he observes that all "these pantomimic gentlemen" will be sent to another state. Only those story tellers will remain who can "imitate the style of the virtuous."

Plato is, at times, just as suspicious of the poets themselves as he is of their work. When he discusses tyrants in the Eighth Book of *The Republic,* he pictures the poets as willing to praise the worst rulers. But the most fundamental objection he has to poets appears in the Tenth Book, and it is derived from his doctrine of ideal forms. In Plato's mind there is an irresolvable conflict between the poet and the philosopher, because the poet imitates only particular objects and is incapable of rising to the first level of abstraction, much less the highest level of ideal forms. True reality, of course, is the ideal, and the poet knows nothing of this; only the philosopher knows the truth.

Poets, moreover, dwell on human passions. And with this point about the passions, we encounter Plato's dualism. The same sort of thinking plays so large a part in both Babbitt and More, that we must examine it in some detail. Plato feels that man has two competing aspects, his rational faculty and his irrational. We can be virtuous only if we control our lower natures, the passions in this case, and strengthen our rational side; and poetry, with all its emphasis on the passions, encourages the audience to give way to emotion. For this reason, then, poetry tends to weaken the power of control, the reason, because it tempts one to indulge his passions, and even the best of men, he maintains, may be corrupted by this subtle influence.

Plato's attitude toward poetry has always been something of an enigma, because he is so completely sensitive to its charm. His whole objection, indeed, seems to rise out of a deep conviction that the poets *do* have great power to influence, but Plato seldom pays any attention to what might be called the poem itself. He is, rather, concerned with the effect on society and he wants the poets to join his fight for justice. He wants them to use their great power to strengthen man's rational side, to teach virtue, and to encourage religion.

While Plato finally allows a few acceptable hymns to the gods and famous men, still he clearly leaves the way open for further discussion of the issue. He even calls upon the poets to defend the Muse and to show that poetry may contribute to virtue. He says:

> We may further grant to those of her [Poetry's] defenders who are lovers of poetry and yet not poets, the permission to speak in prose on her behalf: let them show not only that she is pleasant but also useful to States and to human life, and we will listen in a kindly spirit; for if this can be proved we shall surely be the gainers—I mean, if there is a use in poetry as well as a delight.[1]

When we turn to Aristotle's ideas on the moral measure of literature, it is at once apparent that he is at times equally concerned about the influence of the art. In the ideal state, for instance, he argues that the young citizens should hear only the most carefully selected tales and stories. For this reason, he would banish indecent pictures and speeches from the stage; and the young people should not even be permitted to see comedies till they are old enough to drink strong wine and sit at the public tables. By the time they reach that age, however, Aristotle no longer worries about the evil influence of comedies.

In Aristotle's analysis of tragedy in the *Poetics,* we find an attempt to isolate the art, to consider only those things proper to it, to discover how it differs from other arts, and to deal with the effects peculiar to it. He assures us, early in the *Poetics,* that all art is "imitation" and that all imitation gives pleasure, but he distinguishes between art in general and poetic art on the basis of the means, manner, and the objects of the imitation. Once the poetic arts are separated from the other forms, he lays down his famous definition of tragedy, which sets up standards and so lends direction to the remainder of the work. A tragedy, by his definition, is an imitation of an action that is serious, of a certain magnitude, and complete in itself. It should have a dramatic form with pleasing language, and it should portray incidents which so arouse pity and fear that it purges these emotions in the audience. Any tragedy, he maintains, has six elements: plot, character, and thought (the objects of imitation), diction and melody (the means of imitation), and spectacle (the manner of imitation). Throughout the rest of the *Poetics,* Aristotle continues to discuss the characteristics of these six parts and their interrelationship, and he refers frequently to the standards suggested by his definition of tragedy.

Aristotle's method in the *Poetics,* then, does suggest that we should isolate the work. The Chicago contingent of modern critics follow Aristotle so far in this direction that it is hard to see how they can compare one poem with another for the purpose of evaluation. But there are, however, several features of

Aristotle's approach which open the way for the moral measure of literature. For one thing, Aristotle mentions that plays may corrupt the audience. In addition, his definition of a tragedy invites our attention, because a serious and important action may very well be one that tests the moral fiber of the author or of the characters. And there is one other point in the poetics that invites moral evaluation: Aristotle's notion that the distinctive function of tragedy is to purge one's emotions by arousing pity and fear. He rejects certain plots because they do not contribute to that end. The point is that an ethical critic, with an assist from Freud, can seize on this theory to argue that tragedy provides us with a harmless outlet for our hostile urges. In his study *Samuel Johnson,* Joseph Wood Krutch takes this line when he says that what Aristotle really means by his theory of catharsis is that our evil passions may be so purged by the dramatic ritual that it is "less likely that we shall indulge them through our own acts." In Krutch's view, this is one way to show how literature may be moral in effect without employing the explicit methods of a moralist. And we can add that Krutch's interpretation of purgation is also one answer to Plato's fear that poetry will encourage our passions. If Krutch is correct, tragedy may have quite the opposite effect. It may allay our passions and so restore the rule of reason. Or in more Freudian terms, the experience may serve to sublimate our destructive urges and strengthen the ego and superego.

Gosson and Sidney

The second half of the sixteenth century in England was the setting for a violent and long controversy over the moral quality of renaissance literature, especially the drama. No one suggested that the ethical effects of the art were irrelevant. Both sides agreed that the theater must stand a moral test, but they could not agree on whether the poets were a good or a bad influence. Both sides claimed that Plato and Aristotle supported their cause. Those who wanted to close the theaters, for example, pointed to Plato's *Republic* and those who wished to keep them open called on the Plato of the *Ion* to testify in their behalf.

The most famous document that comes out of this dispute is perhaps Sir Philip Sidney's *An Apologie for Poetrie,* published in 1595. Many students of literature know that classical defense. What is not so well known, however, and what is quite important for understanding the issues of this early quarrel, is the kind of attack on literature that Sidney was answering. For this reason, then, I want to describe, first, two examples of the puritanical attacks: Stephen Gosson's *The School of Abuse,* 1579, and his later *Playes Confuted,* published in 1582. Second, we will see how Sidney answered the charges, for while Sidney's essay was not specifically a reply to Gosson, his arguments do support the new theater.

According to William Ringler's study, *Stephen Gosson,* the theater business in London had become a thriving enterprise by 1577, and, in the opinion of many, a thoroughly bad business. Aroused by what they considered an evil influence, some members of the clergy, joined by city authorities, merchants, and master craftsmen, began the attack on the plays and the actors for what they called "the abuses of the art," but by 1582 some of them began to denounce the whole idea of acting. Although this kind of wholesale objection came at first from some men who were not technically Puritans, still, once the Puritans gained power, they climaxed the affair by passing the infamous ordinance of 1642 which decreed that all "public stage-plays shall cease and be forborne." With that act of Parliament the

21

opponents of the stage won the day, and for more than two decades after that England had no legitimate public drama.

In the early days of this controversy over the theater one of the interested parties, Stephen Gosson, published a little tract in which he objected mildly to the abuses of art, rather than the art itself. But his opposition hardened and by 1579, in *The School of Abuse*, he was ready to banish all "players." He advises women to beware "of those places which in sorrows cheere you and beguile you in mirth." He does not really approve of levity and laughter, but sex is the deadly sin. He warns that a single glance can lead us into temptation, for "Looking eies have lyking hartes, and lyking hartes may burne in lust."

If these references suggest the tone of Gosson's moral code, then it will not be any surprise that Gosson has something of the same ambivalence that one finds in Plato. Gosson's sensitivity to the delights of literature makes him conscious of the good influence it can have. And, in his opinion, there *are* some "good playes and sweete playes" (among them one of his own) which do not offend with amorous gesture. Good modern plays can teach the audience about the greediness of usurers or the danger of false friends, and some ancient poets, too, portray the wholesome counsel of good fathers or the deeds of virtuous men. One may profit by imitating them, but he feels that most of the poets in his own day no longer teach justice or virtue. And the amorous English poets of his own time distribute their poison in the most dangerous form, because they write so beautifully that they easily sell their villainy to an unsuspecting audience. For this reason, he argues, he would side with Plato and banish from the city all poets—good and bad.

Gosson says he aims at plays primarily, but, in fact, he levels actors, audiences, dancers, writers, jugglers, pipers, and jesters. actors, audiences, dancers, writers, jugglers, pipers, and jesters.

22

Not satisfied with the wide range of this fire, he also throws a few random shots at such fellow travelers as "Tumblers," "Dicers," "Carders," and "Fencers." Since he is mostly concerned with the plays, however, he is careful to emphasize that the audiences and the players are a lecherous lot. He argues that all the music, the fine clothes, the effeminate gestures, and the wanton speech of the drama arouse one's sexual desire. He even implies that great empires in the past fell because the theaters demoralized the populace, and he suggests that Englishmen, once strong and masculine, are now growing weak and cowardly. Curiously enough, Gosson does not use the Scriptures to confound his enemies, because he is convinced that he can defeat the poets and the players with the profane writers alone.

By the year 1582, moreover, Gosson's objections had become even more severe. In *Playes Confuted,* he drops any pretense of attacking the abuses of art and objects strenuously to the very idea of drama itself. In William Ringler's opinion, this is one of the most comprehensive attacks on the drama to come out of the Elizabethan or Jacobean periods. Even William Prynne, he says, was unable to add any significant arguments.

The line of argument in *Playes Confuted* is more biblical, more violent, and much closer to the attitudes of the stern Puritan Parliament. Drama, he maintains, is an invention of the devil, dedicated to idolatry. Comedies encourage lust and corruption, and tragedies actually promote cruelty and murder. The plays pretend to be based on fact, but they inevitably distort the truth. The very business of acting itself, pretending to be what one is not, is no better than a lie, and asking boys to take women's parts is directly contrary to the holy Bible.

With several arguments which are pale reminders of Plato, Gosson also objects that drama encourages us into excessive and intemperate shows of emotion. It also tends to take our minds off the spiritual realm and entices us to delight in the mundane.

Thus, Gosson exhibits in *Playes Confuted* many of the narrow religious and moral objections to literary art which were widely held in his day and for years to come. One of the ironies of the controversy is that he dedicated his earlier work, *The School for Abuse*, to Sir Philip Sidney, but the gesture only aroused a masterful opponent, for Sidney entered the literary tournament with his *Apologie* and defended not only the poets, versifiers, and playwriters, but all writers of fiction. Without specifically naming Gosson, Sidney nevertheless answers many of Gosson's wild charges.

After some preliminary sallies designed to show that the Bible itself is poetic, and that poets were greatly honored in ancient times, Sidney lays down the main tenet of his argument: poetry is a form of imitation which can both teach and delight. And he turns Gosson's main point right around when he agrees that the true purpose of all learning is virtue but that poetry has "most served to bring forth" good conduct. Literature is, therefore, the real king of all knowledge.

In Sidney's view there are two other branches of learning which sometimes pretend to the throne of knowledge—ethics and history, but he says that neither one has a valid claim to the highest position. The philosopher, for example, tries to teach with arguments that are so hard to understand that no one really learns the lesson. In fact, Sidney feels that the writing of the philosophers is so difficult and so unimaginative that anyone who actually reads them is already virtuous enough and that those who most need the moral lessons probably never read them.

Sidney argues, further, that the historian is not the best teacher of virtue either, because he must necessarily stay with the actual events rather than deal with what should be.

The poet, however, suffers from neither limitation. Whether he writes in prose or verse, the poet can picture the ideal. He can enliven the philosopher's abstract principles and so decorate virtue that all men fall in love with her. Even if evil characters do appear on the stage, they leave it so manacled that they "little animate folkes to followe them." And the poet reaches a large audience, because he is a "Popular Philosopher." Thus, Sidney claims, the good influence of literature is both wide and deep.

To the stern objection that poets lie, Sidney answers that the real liar is one who affirms what is *not* true. Since the poet affirms nothing, but merely presents *what should be,* he does not lie. To the charge that poetry turns men's minds to "wanton sinfulness and lustful love," Sidney replies that a few artists have misused the art, but that the abuse should not turn us against the good in literature. To Gosson's charge that poetry and plays influence men to turn away from strenuous manly action, Sidney merely answers that the same ignorant objection can be made against all book learning. To the effective argument that Plato banished poets, Sidney replies that Plato merely banished the abuse of poetry, not the thing itself, and he refers to the high praise of poetry in the *Ion* to support his point. Beside this, Plato himself was a poet and interlaced his fictional philosophy with "meere tales, as *Giges* Ring, and others, which who knoweth not to be flowers of Poetries, did never walk into Apollos Garden." Therefore, Sidney proudly claims, Plato is a true patron of the poetic art.

We can leave this controversy by observing that neither Sidney nor Gosson tries to isolate literature; both look to its effect on society. Claiming that literature is the most powerful moral force, Sidney turns Gosson's whole point inside out. While Sidney admits that there are some abuses, he denies that they are so bad that we should banish a potential moral force. It can be said, finally, that Gosson brushes past the Horatian formula with the observation that if a man really wants instruction, there are plenty of ministers around. As he sees it, a man should go to church for moral improvement and he should go to a play for evil entertainment. Sidney, on the other hand, accepts the please-and-teach formula, underscores the instruction side, and claims that literature's power to stir the passions, which so disturbed both Plato and Gosson, is the very quality which makes it such an effective force for good.

Johnson and Hazlitt

With Dr. Johnson and William Hazlitt we have two more critics who are interested in the moral quality of the work, but these two represent diametrically opposite points of view. On one side, Dr. Johnson, the obvious moralist, applauds the rule of reason and the individual who conforms to tradition, and, on the other side, Hazlitt, less obviously the moralist, encourages heightened passions and also applauds the proud, self-willed individual who challenges authority. The striking difference between the two will emerge most clearly if we compare their essays on Milton, paying special attention to their remarks on Milton's remarkable Satan.

Dr. Johnson saw no real conflict of interest between the moralist and the critic. He was just as apt to judge literature by moral standards as he was to measure conduct by the same principles. Indeed, he saw no essential difference between his literary criticism and his general criticism of life. In his *Preface to Shakespeare* he says, "the end of writing is to instruct; the end of poetry is to instruct by pleasing." As Dr. Johnson explains:

> Whether we provide for action or conversation, whether we wish to be useful or pleasing, the first requisite is the

26

religious and moral knowledge of right and wrong; the next is an acquaintance with the history of mankind, and with those examples which may be said to embody truth, and prove by events the reasonableness of opinions. Prudence and justice are virtues and excellences of all times and of all places; we are perpetually moralists, but we are geometricians only by chance. . . . Physiological learning is of such rare emergence, that one man may know another half his life without being able to estimate his skill in hydrostatics or astronomy; but his moral and prudential character immediately appears. Those authors, therefore, are to be read at schools that supply most axioms of prudence, most principles of moral truth, and most materials for conversation; and these purposes are best served by poets, orators and historians. . . . If I have Milton against me, I have Socrates on my side. . . . Socrates was rather of the opinion, that what we had to learn was, how to do good and avoid evil.[2]

It would be a mistake, however, to think that Dr. Johnson has the same sort of deep mistrust of literature that we saw in the Plato of the *Republic* or in Gosson, because Dr. Johnson sees nothing inherently wrong with the art. He was a professional literary man himself and understood and approved of the sort of recreation that fiction might afford, but in his opinion that pleasure was not enough to justify the art. He feels that the finest literature should also promote the good life.

In his work *Samuel Johnson,* Joseph Wood Krutch says that Dr. Johnson was a common sense critic.

Common sense as applied to literature meant, to begin with, the assumption that neither the aims nor the methods of the literary art are peculiar to it. Literature, the assumption is, seeks to give pleasure and to impart instruction; but neither the pleasure it gives nor the instruction it provides constitutes any world apart or requires for its proper appreciation any unique faculties.

27

Johnson, of course, would have been indignantly astonished at anything suggesting the doctrine of the art for art's sake. He would have been equally astonished to hear of "significant form" or an "aesthetic experience." To him sound morality and good sense are the same whether in fact or in fiction, in prose or in verse.[3]

An excellent illustration of Dr. Johnson's "common sense criticism" can be found in the essay on Milton in his *Lives Of The English Poets* (1779-1781). In that discussion he is just as concerned with the moral quality of Milton the man as he is with the moral quality of the art. For example, he condemns the poet for turning against the Presbyterians with the observation that the man who will lightly switch parties "loves himself rather than the truth." But Dr. Johnson's most serious objection to Milton seems to be that the artist has too much individualism. Milton's republicanism, Dr. Johnson feels, issues from an envious hatred of greatness and a sullen desire for inordinate independence. Milton is too impatient with outside control, too disdainful of his superiors. Milton hated monarchs and prelates, Dr. Johnson argues, because he hated anyone he had to obey. Milton wanted to destroy, not establish, and he embraced the cause of liberty only because he despised any kind of authority. In Dr. Johnson's view, Milton betrayed liberty when he stooped to flatter and serve the tyrant Cromwell. And when Milton joined the revolution and defended the execution of the king, then Dr. Johnson loses all respect. He shows no sympathy for Milton, even when the artist falls on evil days "and evil tongues, in darkness and with dangers compassed round." Dr. Johnson comments sternly:

> This darkness, had his eyes been better employed, had undoubtedly deserved compassion: but to add the mention of danger was ungrateful and unjust. He was fallen indeed on *evil days*; the time was come in which regicides could

no longer boast their wickedness. But of *evil tongues* for Milton to complain, required impudence at least equal to his other powers; Milton whose warmest advocates must allow that he never spared any asperity of reproach or brutality of insolence.[4]

Despite the fact that Dr. Johnson condemns Milton the man, he does not condemn the poet. He does not confuse the two, for many of Milton's poems teach important moral truths in "the most affecting manner." In *Paradise Lost,* for example, Dr. Johnson observes that history gave the poet the basic narrative, but the artist's own moral sense makes the poem truly great. He likes the fact that Satan's rebellious sentiments do not taint the reader's imagination. As he says, "there is in Satan's speeches little that can give pain to a pious ear." And he claims that Milton's moral sentiments excel those of all other poets, with every line of *Paradise Lost* fairly breathing the purest sanctity of thought and manner. When he turns to *Comus,* Dr. Johnson comments favorably on the fact that the invitations to pleasure in that work are so abstractly stated that they contain no distinct and carnal images to corrupt the reader's mind.

But Dr. Johnson realizes that too much moral instruction can be a bore and that the author who goes too far can lose his audience. He feels, for example, that *Comus* is "tediously instructive" and that even the magnificent *Paradise Lost* can be more of a duty than a pleasure. As he puts it:

> We read Milton for instruction, retire harassed and over-burdened, and look elsewhere for recreation; we desert our master and seek for companions.[5]

I suppose we can say, then, that Dr. Johnson's famous common sense urges him to call a halt to too much moralizing. At least it is clear that he really means it when he subscribes to

29

both sides of the Horatian equation, for he seldom forgets that literature must please as well as teach. And in one rare and morally neutral mood he even approves of literature which does not teach anything at all:

> There are, in the present state of things, so many more instigations to evil, than incitements to good, that he who keeps me in a neutral state, may be justly considered as a benefactor to life.[6]

With William Hazlitt's *Lectures on the English Poets* (1818-1819), we move into a different age and encounter different attitudes. If we look at his remarks on Milton and also at his poetic theory in "On Poetry in General," the first lecture in the group, we can see just how far Hazlitt is from Dr. Johnson.

The first thing to notice is that the very style as well as the intent of their criticism is different. Dr. Johnson is analytic; Hazlitt is impressionistic. Dr. Johnson moves sedately from one part of the work to the next (from the plot to the sentiments, to the characters, and then to the style), but Hazlitt skips lightly from one aspect to another. Hazlitt thinks that the best criticism should "reflect the colours, the light and shade, the soul and the body of a work" and his essays do indeed reflect many facets which fascinate him. In fact, the order of his essays follows his enthusiasm rather than any formal plan.

In his own way, nonetheless, Hazlitt is as much the moral critic as Dr. Johnson. He pays lip service to the notion that poetry should appeal to the whole man: his sensitivity (the power to feel), his intellect (the desire to know), and his moral sense (the will to act). But the characteristic which most concerns the critic is the fact that poetry appeals to our sensitivity. He dwells on the intense passions and images which poetry can arouse in either the audience or the poet himself. He says at the outset of his lectures:

30

The best general notion which I can give of poetry is, that it is the natural impression of any object or event, by its vividness exciting an involuntary movement of imagination and passion, and producing by sympathy, a certain modulation of the voice, or sounds expressing it.[7]

For Hazlitt, poetry is an exciting sense of beauty, a power that "is high-wrought enthusiasm of fancy and feeling." The final test of poetry is the intensity of its effect, and the subject matter must help to convey this extraordinary impulse to the imagination. In short, the best poem will encourage the random and violent movements of our passions. That, for him, is the goal. The free exercise of our feelings, rather than their control, now becomes the good. This is, of course, merely Plato's point about the passions in reverse.

Looking for passages which would arouse his feelings, Hazlitt finds much that pleases him in *Paradise Lost*. He regards it as essentially a "poem of passion."

I shall say nothing of the fable, or of other technical objections or excellences; but I shall try to explain at once the foundation of the interest belonging to the poem. . . . In a word, the interest of the poem arises from the daring ambition and fierce passions of Satan, and from the account of the paradisiacal happiness, and the loss of it by our first parents. Three-fourths of the work are taken up with these characters, and nearly all that relates to them is unmixed sublimity and beauty.[8]

Hazlitt notices the intense bliss of Adam and Eve before the fall; he remarks on the loss of "unspeakable happiness and resignation to inevitable fate." But Satan is the one who catches his attention as the most admirable character in the work. He calls Satan "the most heroic subject that was ever chosen for a poem, and the execution is as perfect as the design is lofty." Hazlitt is impressed by Satan's great fortitude, his

31

strength of mind, his power of action, and his fierce, intemperate emotions. With Satan's love of power, his pride and self-will, and his struggle for unattainable ends, Hazlitt feels that Milton has drawn a superior creature who is dazzlingly splendid even in defeat.

Hazlitt's interest in poems which excite the passions and his praise for Milton's dark prince are familiar principles in the early nineteenth century, and they provide a remarkable contrast to Dr. Johnson. In the next pair of critics we shall look at, we will find the same sort of conflict of interest, and in Oscar Wilde we encounter Hazlitt's emotionalism carried to an extreme.

Arnold and Wilde

With Oscar Wilde we are in the middle of the nineteenth century revolt against the conventionally moral critic. Wilde takes the position that literary art, properly understood, has nothing to do with ethics, because it has nothing to do with action. In his view there is not really a mass audience, only the isolated individual enjoying a high and creative heat. Now, clearly, if one does nothing but emote over a poem, that sort of inactivity is just as much conduct as any other kind, so we can say that Wilde, too, in his unconventional way, advocates an ethic. A peculiarly aesthetic ethic to be sure, but an ethic nonetheless. But his picture of the good life is so solipsistic and so limited that it is contrary to the main stream of the moral concern for literature.

Matthew Arnold, on the other hand, continues in the older tradition of the critic who feels that literature should somehow improve us and that we must measure greatness in the art by moral standards. Arnold shies away from the Horatian idea that literature should please and instruct. Instead, he is fond of saying that the greatest art gives us "a criticism of life." That general phrase covers all kinds of literary and moral values, but we shall concentrate only on those features of the principle which are especially relevant to our concern.

In "Literature and Science" in his *Discourses In America* (1885), Arnold asserts that man has a strong desire to integrate his knowledge, his "sense for beauty," and his "sense for conduct." In that desire for unity lies the strength of the "hold which letters have upon us." When we feel the impulse to integrate our knowledge with our sense for conduct or with our sense for beauty, we are revealing our desire for good, our desire that good should be forever present.

The important question, then, for understanding Arnold, is to find what will help us achieve the unity of personality which leads to the good life. Science can not do it, Arnold thinks, because science can only increase our knowledge, not relate it to action. But both religion and poetry can help, because both have great power to engage our emotions. Since the middle ages, however, religion has weakened as a force in our lives and this slow attenuation has steadily increased the need for poetry, because through its evaluation of experience, poetry can help us relate new knowledge to our need for beauty and for better conduct. "Poetry attaches its emotion to the idea; the idea *is* the fact. The strongest part of our religion today is its unconscious poetry," says Arnold. He thinks that good poetry can console and sustain us, and "the consolation and the stay will be . . . in proportion to the power of the criticism of life."

In Arnold's opinion, we all have some sort of moral and aesthetic thirst which can best be satisfied by good literature, and when it is so satisfied we will be better men. Arnold does not go into any detail to show just how the art performs this important function, but he is utterly convinced that it does.

Despite this heavy moral emphasis, Arnold disapproves of narrow and explicit moralizing. In his essay on "Wordsworth" (1879), for example, he maintains that when Voltaire says that "no nation has treated in poetry moral ideas with more energy and depth than the English nation," he was not suggesting that the English excel in didactic poems, but rather that they excel in the noble and profound application of ideas to life under the conditions fixed by the laws of poetic beauty and poetic truth.

> If it is said that to call these ideas moral ideas is to introduce a strong and injurious limitation, I answer that it is to do nothing of the kind, because moral ideas are really so main a part of human life. The question *how to live,* is itself a moral idea; and it is the question which most interests every man, and with which, in some way or other, he is perpetually occupied.[9]

Arnold wants the term "moral" to have a "large sense," as he calls it, and in that sense, he feels, English poetry does reveal an energetic and profound treatment of moral ideas. If the poet is to apply *the best ideas* to life, then what we really mean is *the best moral ideas*, "because human life itself is in so preponderating a degree moral." While Arnold admits that we might occasionally enjoy poetry which attacks morality or is indifferent to it, still he insists that poetry which revolts against moral ideas is really revolting against life itself and poetry which is indifferent to morality is actually indifferent to life. The final value of poetry is far beyond any beauty of style or argument, and anyone who mistakes these pretty virtues for the ultimate value is like a man who stays in a pleasant inn when he ought to get on home to attend to duty. And only the virtuous enjoy real "serenity, happiness, and contentment." In a single sentence, Arnold puts it this way:

It is important, therefore, to hold fast to this: that poetry is at botton a criticism of life; that the greatness of a poet lies in his powerful and beautiful application of ideas to life—to the question: How to live.[10]

If the art is to have this high moral quality, then the artist must have a mind of the same high quality and that sort of mind would necessarily be moral. In the best writers, therefore, he looks for a "high seriousness born of absolute sincerity." Both Burns and Chaucer, in his opinion, lack this virtue. "The substance of Chaucer's poetry, his view of things and his criticism of life has largeness, freedom, shrewdness, benignity; but it does not have the high seriousness." Chaucer has exquisite style and manner, but he does not rank with Shakespeare, Homer, or Dante because of this failing. And Arnold adds that "Burns, like Chaucer, comes short of the high seriousness of the great classics, and the virtue of matter and manner which goes with that seriousness is wanting in his work."

But there is one curious turn in Arnold's theory, and it attracts Oscar Wilde. Arnold thinks that the literary critic in the broadest sense of the term should not become personally embroiled in "the region of immediate practice, in the political, social, humanitarian sphere," if he wants to achieve the free, speculative treatment of things so necessary for the spiritual and intellectual health of the culture. English criticism, he regrets, has been too polemical and too controversial. It has dealt so much with narrowly practical questions that it has not succeeded in establishing an order of the best ideas which will nourish the creative spirit. When there is such a climate of opinion, such a fund of ideas, then the literary artist will turn to the noble and significant actions of his own day or those of other periods for his subjects and such subjects can powerfully and delightfully affect what is "permanent in the human soul." And for all of this, the true critic should prepare the way.

On the surface there seems to be an immeasurable distance between the attitudes of Arnold and those of the aesthete Oscar Wilde, but the strange truth is that Wilde agrees with Arnold on several points and relies on them to support his "art for art's sake" point of view. Paul Elmer More argues that the relation between Arnold and Wilde is a natural consequence of Arnold's inadequacies. What disturbs More is that Arnold has such a flimsy notion of the relation of the aesthetic and the moral that he leaves criticism "subject to a one-sided and dangerous development." And Paul Elmer More refers, of course, to Oscar Wilde's emphasis on the emotional and narrowly aesthetic values of the art rather than on the moral quality. In More's mind Arnold unwittingly preached "the religion of taste."

If Arnold did help to father Wilde, the issue is a curious irony of paternity, because Wilde works himself into almost complete isolation from the total culture that Arnold was so interested in. In *The Critic As Artist* Wilde argues that real thought is impaired by association with actual practice, that one can not form a disinterested judgment if he is engaged in the affairs of men. Wilde, like Arnold, broadens the term *critic* to include the observer who has a general intellectual curiosity and judgment, and he, too, believes that criticism helps to create the intellectual atmosphere of the age. Wilde also applauds Arnold's theory that there is a critical element in all creative work, but he goes on to say that the critic is even more creative than the artist. In Arnold, the critical spirit is judicial, helping to determine the best that has been thought and said, but in Wilde the critical spirit becomes a self-conscious and highly sensitive response to art. The highest criticism, he feels, is a record of one's personal impressions, a record of the sensitive soul's experience with the masterpiece. If the critic's sole aim is "to chronicle his own impressions," then the art object is the starting point for a new and quite personal creation. And that is exactly what Wilde wants.

In a kind of caricature of Arnold's idea that the critic should not get involved in petty quarrels, Wilde pictures the critic as so completely detached from life that he withdraws into a world of pure art, actually turning to art for experience rather than to the world. In this art realm he can freely exercise his emotions, for art is *of* emotion, *by* emotion and *for* emotion— *not* action. The proper cultivation of this Wilde version of the "critical spirit" can free our imagination, and free us from the "self-imposed and trammelling burden of moral responsibility." He pictures the aesthetic critic in the following words:

> Calm and self centered, and complete, the aesthetic critic contemplates life . . . . He has discovered how to live.
>
> Is such a mode of life immoral? Yes: all the arts are immoral, except those baser forms of sensual or didactic art that seek to excite to action of evil or of good. For action of every kind belongs to the sphere of ethics. The aim of art is simply to create a mood.[11]

Of course Wilde is a professional nonconformist who loves to shock Victorian sensibilities, but he is also serious when he argues that the critic should be neither fair nor sincere, because those qualities are "if not actually moral, at least, on the border land of morals, and the first condition of criticism is that the critic should" see that the spheres of art and ethics are absolutely separate. The Puritan critics kill beauty, he declares, for beauty is beyond morality. Art is, in fact, beyond everything in the ordinary world, for the artist does not copy life, he creates it. Thus, truth in art is style, or "one's last mood," and has nothing to do with the subject of the piece. As he explains:

> As long as a thing is useful or necessary to us . . . or is a vital part of the environment in which we live, it is outside the proper sphere of art. To art's subject matter we should be more or less indifferent.[12]

Wilde issues all his observations without any pretense of finality. In general, he is sceptical about the possibility of capturing any unchanging truths, but he says that he loves his provisional truths for their own sake, just as if they were absolutes. The critic simply searches for truth among his own moods and emotions. The motto for this approach might well be "Every man for himself," because no matter what the issue, everyone is on his own. If literature does help "common natures seek to realize their own perfection," that is merely an accidental effect and is completely irrelevant to either the creation of the art or its appreciation. Art is important because it gives the individual artist and the critic a chance for self expression. The value of the art is private.

This sort of talk is, of course, evaluative. These are normative principles and can lead to specific judgments. Wilde tries to persuade us to accept his set of values, his aesthetic version of the good life, but if one points out that he is a moralizer of a sort, he will protest that he has no such intention. We have in Wilde something of a semantic problem, and we should not be surprised when he shies away from such traditional ethical terms as *virtue*. "Virtue!" he will snort. "Who knows what the virtues are? Not you, not I." But the truth is that he argues for the value of the aesthetic experience, as he understands that experience, and it is morally good.

One last point about Wilde is worth our notice: his relation with another critic of his time, Walter Pater. There are many reflections of Pater in Wilde's essays. He says, for example, that Pater's well known meditation on the Mona Lisa is "criticism of the highest kind," because it treats the art as a jump-

38

ing off point for a new creation. And he frankly adopts Pater's hedonistic pursuit of the vivid stirring of mind and body. Wilde listens closely when Peter advises the art lover to burn with a "hard, gemlike flame," to cultivate the delicate and exquisite passions that make for ecstasy.

The experience of art for both Wilde and Pater has obvious sexual overtones. They urge us to woo art in the hope that we can experience an aesthetic orgasm. "Life has such sinful brevity," Pater warns, that we should gather rosebuds while we may. He describes his love:

> Of such wisdom, the poetic passion, the desire of beauty, the love of art for its own sake, has most. For art comes to you proposing frankly to give nothing but the highest quality to your moments as they pass, and simply for the moments' sake.[18]

But let there be no mistake. Pater is not Wilde. They certainly agree about the quality of the art experience, but Pater wants art to serve a moral, even a religious end. As he does with Arnold, so here, Wilde simply picks out what suits his own taste, for Pater added serious qualifications to his doctrine of art for art's sake. The best of art, Pater argues, will bring a better moral life. He maintains that

> the distinction between great art and good art [depends] immediately, as regards literature at all events, not on its form, but on the matter. Thackeray's *Esmond*, surely, is greater art than *Vanity Fair*, by the greater dignity of its interests. It is on the quality of the matter it informs or controls, its compass, its variety, its alliance to great ends . . . that the greatness of literary art depends, as *The Divine Comedy, Paradise Lost, Les Miserables*, The English *Bible*, are great art. Given the conditions I have tried to explain as constituting good art;—then, if it be devoted further to the increase of men's happiness, to the redemption of the oppressed, or the enlargement of our

39

sympathies with each other, or to such presentment of new or old truth about ourselves and our relation to the world as may ennoble and fortify us in our sojourn here, or immediately, as with Dante, to the glory of God, it will be also great art; if, over and above . . . that colour and mystic perfume, and that reasonable structure, it has something of the soul of humanity in it, and finds its logical, its architectural place, in the great structure of human life.[14]

Evidently Wilde was so fascinated with the colorful sensations in Pater's criticism that he paid no attention to the insistence on the close relation between art and action.

Lowell and Poe

In some ways James Russell Lowell and Edgar Allan Poe seem to be the American counterparts of Arnold and Wilde. Lowell, for one, is as firm as Arnold in his contention that the best literature makes better men. As he puts it, in his essay on Wordsworth, "no great poet has ever sung, but the whole human race has been, sooner or later, the wiser and better for it."

And Poe seems just as anxious as Wilde is to separate literature from the general life. The promise of poetry is beauty, says Poe; and beauty, for Poe, is a psychological state very much like Wilde's heightened emotion. The contrast between Lowell and Poe, then, seems clear enough, but the closer we look at Poe's critical theory and at his actual literary judgments, the more the contrast fades, and we are finally left with the feeling that Poe did not have as much understanding of the issues as Wilde did.

Lowell's criticism, on the other hand, is quite consistent and in the grand manner. For him the poet retains enough of his ancient priestly role so that his function is still essentially moral, even religious. The poet is the inspired "seer" who can look beyond the changing world of particular things on into the unchanging spiritual realm of ideal forms. As Lowell puts it:

> The poet is he who can best say and see what is ideal—what belongs to the world of soul and of beauty . . . . He is the revealer of Deity . . . . He does not always directly rebuke what is bad and base, but indirectly by making us feel what delight there is in the good and the fair . . . . Whoever reads the great poets cannot but be made better by it, for they always introduce him to a higher society, to a greater style of manners and thinking. Whoever learns to love what is beautiful is made incapable of the low and mean and bad.[15]

Clearly, then, the poet's duty is to exalt men's minds, to give "right direction and safe outlet to their passion through imagination," and to help their sense of proportion, form, and ultimately their ability to adjust means to ends. If the poet has the pleasant task of setting our lives to music, he must also purify and enlighten the audience. The poet should define our duty and then encourage us to perform it.

But Lowell is aware that all morality and no manner makes a dull poem. He wants the poet inspired enough to come close to a perfection of verbal form, but if the artist is to be a great poet, then he must also know the truth. He praises Keats, for instance, because he thinks the English writer possesses "the divine faculty" in equal measure with a "vigorous understanding," so that the most perfect music and meaning float together in his poems. But a lesser poet, like Wordsworth, is too much the pedagogue and too often forgets that poetry should never instruct by plain precept or by openly insisting on a moral. Even as a critic, Lowell feels, Wordsworth pays too little attention to "those subsidiary qualities which make . . . [poetry] the charmer of leisure and the employment of minds without definite objects." While Lowell would probably agree that a

41

man "groping in the dark passages of life" might come upon some axiom in literature which would help him get his bearings, still poetry should teach by "inducing a mood rather than enforcing a . . . moral." The primary object of tragedy, then, is not to moralize in any formal sense. Rather, as Lowell expresses it:

> The moral office of tragedy is to show us our own weaknesses idealized in grander figures and more awful results— to teach us that what we pardon in ourselves as venial faults . . . have arms as long as those of kings, and reach forward to the catastophe of our lives . . . so that if we should be brought to the test of a great temptation or a stringent emergency we must be involved in a ruin as sudden and complete as that we shudder at in the unreal scene of the theater . . . . Representing life, it [tragedy] teaches, like life, by indirection, by those nods and winks that are thrown away on us blind horses in such profusion.[16]

Thus, it makes no real difference to Lowell whether the artist has a *moral purpose* or not. Shakespeare, for example, has no moral aim at all, and yet, as Lowell says:

> with temperament so just, an insight so inevitable as his, it was impossible that the moral reality, which underlies the *mirage* of the poet's vision, should not always be suggested.[17]

Shakespeare's plays, therefore, lead a public life that is independent of the author, and we can learn from *Lear*, for instance, how to distinguish between "a wise generosity and a loose handed weakness of giving" or we may learn from *Macbeth* how one sin can involve us in another.

Lowell's conception of the function of the literary critic closely parallels Arnold's ideas on that score. Everything connected with great literature is terribly noble, and the critic, too, is "set apart to a kind of priesthood. He is the appointed guardian of the ideal in art and life." In short, the critic is the aesthetic-moralist on the grandest scale, the only one who really knows the best that has been thought and said.

If one picks the passages carefully, Poe will seem to disagree with Lowell and, indeed, he may sound like Oscar Wilde. Poe argues, for instance, that it is wrong to judge poetry by moral standards. He protests vigorously against what he calls "the didactic heresy." In *The Poetic Principle,* 1848, he puts it this way:

> Every poem, it is said, should inculcate a moral; and by this moral is the poetical merit of the work to be adjudged. . . . We have taken it into our heads that to write a poem simply for the poem's sake, and to acknowledge such to have been our design, would be to confess ourselves radically wanting in the true Poetic dignity and force:—but the simple fact is, that, would we but permit ourselves to look into our own souls, we should immediately there discover that under the sun there exists nor can exist any work more thoroughly dignified—more supremely noble than this very poem—this poem *per se*—this poem which is a poem and nothing more—this poem written solely for the poem's sake.[18]

Poe tries to distinguish between our concern for truth, morality and beauty, and the poet, he says, hopes to satisfy our thirst for beauty. In contrast, our intellectual faculty aims at truth. The proper medium for the intellect is prose, not verse, and the proper creative mood is "the exact converse of the poetical": one should be "cool, calm and unimpassioned."

Our moral sense, Poe thinks, is concerned with duty, with conduct. Reason may assist the moral sense, but conscience is its guide. Beauty, however, is significantly different from other aspects, for our aesthetic "taste" searches for beauty, and poetry is a perfect source for such satisfaction. And beauty, for him, is really a special kind of psychological effect the art has on the individual. Beauty, in fact, is much like Wilde's or Pater's impassioned state. As Poe explains:

> When, indeed, men speak of Beauty, they mean, precisely, not a quality, as is supposed, but an effect—they refer, in short, just to that intense and pure elevation of soul—not of intellect, or of the heart— . . . which is experienced in consequence of contemplating "the beautiful."[19]

In the act of creation the artist himself experiences the same sort of "shivering delight" that the reader ought to feel. And if the critic wants to measure the beauty of a work, he must somehow measure the intensity of his feelings. Perhaps the best known of Poe's critical theories, that a poem should be short, follows from his identification of beauty with intense feeling. Poe reasons that our moments of "intense excitement are, through psychal necessity, brief." Thus, if the beauty of a poem is the emotional excitement it can induce, and if that is necessarily short lived, then truly successful poems are necessarily short. They last only long enough to stimulate the emotions and then stop. So-called long epic poems, in Poe's opinion, are really only shorter pieces tied together by rather dull prosaic passages in between. And, needless to add, mere truth or the call to duty is not exciting enough to bring on the poetic state; and any poem which aims *mainly* at either intellectual or moral truths is bound to be a pseudo-poem after all.

We must be clear, however, that Poe does not rule moral or intellectual truth entirely out of poetry. He does not want to bar them altogether, so much as he wants to make sure that they are subordinate to beauty. In the *Philosophy of Composition*, for instance, he assures us that truth may profitably be introduced into the work, for it can help achieve the poetic effect. And in *The Poetic Principle,* he agrees that moral precepts, as well as truths, may properly enter the poem, but the true artist will be careful to see that these elements are subordinate to "Beauty which is the atmosphere and the real essence of the poem."

And this brings us to a curious inconsistency in Poe's understanding of "Beauty." When he really gets going on his theory of the poetic mood, he makes it sound like a moment of religious inspiration, almost a trance. He calls it a time when one enjoys the "ecstatic prescience of the glories beyond the grave," the angelic music of the "beauty above." And this sort of inspiration is apparently the same for the poet at the moment of creation as it is for the audience at the moment of appreciation. But it is hard to reconcile all these high sounding words with Poe's own account of writing his most popular poem, *The Raven.* In that essay, Poe seems so far from an impassioned state that he is in a perfect mood for prose: "cool, calm and unimpassioned." He frankly lets us look behind the scenes "at the elaborate and vacillating crudities of thought . . . at the wheels and pinions—the tackle for scene-shifting the step-ladders and demon-tarps—the cock's feathers, the red paint and block patches" which constitute the true business of poetic composition. In fact, Poe makes fun of poets who would have us believe that they compose in a "fine frenzy of ecstatic intuition" and he leaves the impression that he never touches the stuff himself.

But the most striking difficulty in Poe's ideas about the moral quality of literature is that several of the poems which appear as illustrations in *The Poetic Principle,* and poems which he praised highly, are *openly* and *obviously* didactic, so much so, in fact, that Lowell himself would probably object. Lowell does complain about Wordsworth's didacticism and he could just as easily object to the openly moral tone of Thomas Hood's

Bridge of Sighs. In that work Hood attacks the "cold inhumanity" of a society which drives a girl to suicide. Poe evidently likes the poem because it deals with the death of a beautiful girl, one of his favorite poetic subjects, but it is also interesting that he does not mind the heavy moralizing. He says, further, that Byron's *Stanzas to Augusta* are a fine expression of the noble idea "that no man can consider himself entitled to complain of Fate while, in his adversity, he still retains the unwavering love of woman." When he praises this "noble theme," he pays tribute to the moral values in the work. Again Poe praises the sincerity, the ideal quality in a didactic poem by Nathaniel P. Willis. This work compares the motives of two women: one marries for money and the other freely gives herself for love. The first girl, Willis explains, is honored by society while the second is cursed, and the poet observes that society's moral condemnation of the second girl is wrong and that Christ would certainly have forgiven her whose "woman's heart gave way." To be sure, the morality is not exactly Sunday School ethics, but it is a moral lesson nonetheless.

It may be that Poe objects to didactic poems only when they preach a doctrine not his own, or it may be that even in these poems Poe feels that morality is properly subservient. In any case, the poems he praises in this essay are so didactic that one wonders what he means when he talks about the "didactic heresy."

As I said at the opening of this section, our sampling of critics is not a history of literary criticism, but it does suggest one fact which the history of criticism also confirms: that the protest against measuring literature by its moral effect is a relatively late development. We have agreed that even Oscar Wilde is a moral critic of a kind, because he judges by his own unusual ethic, but men like Wilde and Poe, in theory at least,

46

want the art to have value for its own sake, separate from its effect on the general life. The older pattern, in the Western World, however, is on the side of the ethical critic.

This departure from the long tradition which appeared in the nineteenth century raises the question of why it occurred. Not why it occurred at that particular time, but why it occurred at all. There are at least three reasons which seem relevant.

For one thing, the anti-moral critics were probably motivated by the mass movement toward specialization in all fields that began in the early modern period. In the middle ages, for instance, there was no great danger from over-specialization, because no one discipline, in the medieval period, could declare its independence of the others. Everyone accepted the notion that theology and ethics properly outranked the other fields. But one of the early signs of the new era was the desire for intellectual independence. Natural science began to break away from religion, and then branches within the new science separated from the others. Literature was also deeply influenced by this same movement. Drama left the church, and the Gosson-Sidney controversy is a reflection of the argument over that early break. While the move away from church domination does not necessarily lead to the separation of literature from the general life, still the later development is at least a continuation of the early interest in specialization.

And those who hoped to specialize in the creation and enjoyment of poetry also tried to bolster the sagging status of the art by claiming that poetry was uniquely important—not only special, but better than all the rest. The rhythm, the precision of expression, the imagery—all these were said to be unique features. The old Platonic idea that the poet is a "seer" was polished up and put into service to prove his unique importance. Of course, anyone who claims that poetry is unique

47

does not have to separate it from the general life. As we have seen, critics like Arnold and Lowell argued that poetry made a unique contribution to good conduct, but it does open the way for others, like Wilde, to claim that poetry was unique because it was beyond ethics and somehow an end in itself.

And one other tendency which must have influenced the anti-ethical critics was the emphasis on the private and passionate effect of art, both in creation and appreciation. The treasured "end in itself," the art, became an excited state. And there was also the implication that this intense appreciation was beyond the reach of the common herd. Only the very best people could enjoy it, so that the shrinking audience was said to prove the superiority of the art. Thus, those who took this view argued that we might have better living, through poetry, for a precious few. In short, they emphasized the emotional and private aspects of art, rather than the more rational and public features.

In contrast to these anti-ethical critics, the men of this study, Babbitt, More, and Winters, all continue the older tradition of those who are interested in the public role of literature: they are ethical critics. Let us turn now to the first of the trio, Irving Babbitt, to see how he met the problems of the moral measure of literature.

CHAPTER III

Irving Babbitt

Irving Babbitt aimed at so much more than most literary critics do that it is sometimes difficult to think of him as one at all. Of course, he had an interest in literature, but he was a social critic in the largest sense of the word, engaged in a serious struggle with an evil that threatened to destroy western civilization. With all the gloomy religious fervor of an early Protestant, he reminds us that our lives are already a kind of hell on earth and that our civilization is headed straight toward dissolution and final death. As he puts it:

> No more delirious spectacle has ever been witnessed than that of hundreds of millions of human beings using a vast machinery of scientific efficiency to turn life into a hell for one another . . . . The dissolution of civilization with which we are threatened is likely to be worse in some respects than that of Greece or Rome in view of the success that has been attained in "perfecting the mystery of murder."[1]

But Babbitt was no real puritan: the death of civilization was not "predetermined" and there were no "elect." In fact, Babbitt felt that he knew the causes of all our ills and how to correct them. The basic trouble was that we had gone "wrong on first principles" and if we went right on first principles, *individually,* then we might all be saved. That was the challenge as he saw it, and he accepted it and spent his vast energy and all his life working for that secular salvation.

Babbitt actually began his struggle before 1900, but he fought relatively alone under the banner of Humanism till the late twenties when he began to attract a few followers. By 1930 the dispute over Neo-Humanism had grown so considerable that one historian comments "in both bulk and bitterness, [it] rivalled the controversy over the economic depression." The depression, indeed, brought attention to Babbitt's cause. He had been around for a long time, gloomily predicting disaster, and the depression seemed to be the end of everything. At least, people were more willing to listen in those dark times, and Babbitt was anxious to be heard. He had plenty to say.

By now, however, the heat of that particular controversy over Neo-Humanism has cooled, and I do not want to pick among the ashes. What I wish to do, instead, is to focus on Babbitt the literary critic, and to evaluate him in that role. Of course, it is not easy to separate Babbitt the social critic from Babbitt the literary critic, because he never separated the social problems from the literary ones. How then can we focus on Babbitt the critic? The strict truth is that it can not be done without giving a false impression of his views. What we will try to do is to look at some of Babbitt's first principles, his ethical axioms, and then see how he fashioned each of them into a critical principle. In a second part of this section we shall turn to some of Babbitt's actual judgments to see just how he employed his principles. In so far as Babbitt's discourse will allow, we will concentrate on his critical theory and practice.

The Theory

One of Babbitt's central ideas is that we must never divorce literature from the general life. At the beginning of *The New Laokoön* he says that an inquiry into the nature of literary genres necessarily ramifies out in every direction and involves ultimately "one's attitude not merely toward literature but life." The chief problem for both society and literature, as he sees it, is that man has lost sight of the eternal truths of dualism and the possibility of ethical effort through individual control by the will. The terms he employs to describe the evils of society are often the same as those he uses to point out faults in literature. If literature is impressionistic, it is because man has no "center," no sense of anything permanent that he can oppose to the flux of phenomena and the torrent of impressions. If confusion has crept into literature, then that confusion itself is merely a special aspect of a more general malady, naturalism. When Babbitt discusses Rousseau, for instance, he debates what he feels are the main issues of contemporary life in literature, politics, education, and religion. If men do change, if they ever learn what he calls "decorum" (exercise of control), then they will enjoy literature which is itself decorous. They will then turn to the writings of the ancients or to the poetry of Goethe's classical period.

The most important person in any society, moreover, is the philosopher. It is his job to find unifying principles to oppose to the flux of relativism. It is his job to oppose individual caprice by solving the general problem of standards for conduct.

The literary critic, Babbitt feels, plays a smaller role, for he deals with one manifestation of the larger evil. The critic is to play second fiddle to the philosopher, but he is to play the same tune, for the critic is to oppose individual caprice in art by upholding artistic standards. In his review of George Saints-bury's *A History of English Criticism,* he observes that a critic should be tolerant enough to embrace all modes of literary expression and should not be a moralist in any one-sided or mechanical sense. The true critic should have the spiritual perception of an Emerson and the aesthetic sensitivity of a

Keats. But Babbitt roundly damns what he calls "aesthetics," "the intense inane," whenever it is divorced from ethics. Any critic who is primarily concerned with the aesthetic features of a work is guilty of a grave philosophical error. The critic is to take his cue from the philosopher and act "as a moderating influence on the opposite insanities between which mankind in the lump is constantly tending to oscillate."

It is clear enough that the philosopher and his cohort the critic are to measure life and literature by moral standards. But what standards? A short answer is "dualism," the "levels of experience" an dthe "inner check." Those three ideas, in one form or another, appear on almost every page of his writings, no matter what the subject, and that constancy is what gives his work such extraordinary unity. He has a few master ideas which he repeats in endlessly diversified language. As Paul Elmer More says, "There is something almost inhuman in the immobility of his central ideas." More observes further that Babbitt is "inclined to crowd his whole thesis, at least implicitly, into each single paragraph, so that the book, despite the inexhaustible variety of his illustrations, gives the impression of endless repetition." It is true that Babbitt loves to illustrate his points by passing rapidly from one age, one country, one language to another, but he always comes back to one of his master ideas: dualism, the levels of experience, or the power of the will guided by the law of measure.

First, then, the basic idea behind Babbitt's dualism is an ancient distinction between *The One* (the permanent) and *The Many* (the changing). He habitually understands and organizes his experience with that contrast in mind. To be sure, the idea may appear in many different pairs of contrasting terms, but they all derive their meaning ultimately from the difference between the One and the Many. To illustrate something of the many forms his dualism can take, he may refer to the fixed (the one) as opposed to the changing (the many); the absolute as opposed to the relative; the unity of things as opposed to the flux; the permanent as opposed to the unstable; the spirit as opposed to the thing; law of spirit as opposed to the law of the members; human progress as opposed to natural progress; or the soul as opposed to the body.

In theory Babbitt insists that he avoids either extreme: over-emphasis on the One or on the Many. He feels that he holds a well balanced position between the two, championing a "one-ness that is always changing." And this sounds much like good academic objectivity, but Babbitt is not neutral at all. He is a rabid partisan, a moralist, and a determined one at that! His dualism is no mere distinction; it is a normative principle, an ethical standard. He feels that he must praise the permanent and fight against the flux, because modern society is out of balance. Modern society accepts only the changing, so he is obliged to restore the balance by supporting the One against the Many. Thus, the One is for him "good" and the Many is "evil."

In Babbitt's thinking, man, like everything else, is dual. He has two aspects: a higher nature (good), and a lower nature (evil). As before, the idea can best be illustrated by listing some of the contrasting terms which reflect the basic dichotomy; man's power of vital control as opposed to his power of sym-pathy, man's head as opposed to his heart, man's masculine as opposed to his feminine nature, man's insight as opposed to his instinct, man's higher will as opposed to his expansive will, man's soul as opposed to his body.

Babbitt's "levels of experience" is another normative prin-ciple that is close to his dualism. There are three levels of experience, the religious, the human, and the lower animal level, and Babbitt urges us to occupy the human level and to eschew the bestial. While he advocates no ordinary religious

53

view, still he stresses the value of religion. His reasoning seems to be that the church has for so long been the guardian of ethics, that we can not attack the church without weakening morality too. In fact, the church has had a monopoly on the higher life for so long a time that even to separate church from state incurs the risk of separating the state from morality as well.

Now both Babbitt's dualism and his levels of experience are important standards in his literary criticism. If he splits the world and man into two, he does precisely the same thing with literary art. He is fond of saying that the true critic should define "inductively," but induction means little more than to separate the worthy features of the art from the less worthy characteristics. For example, there is always the "inner form," the paraphrasable content, which he calls the "soul of art," as opposed to the mere "outer form," or technique. Of course, "soul" here is a highly evaluative term, and the implication is that "inner form" is the *essence* of literature and technique is somehow *peripheral*. To his mind, any poem should stand primarily on the quality of its inner form, but Babbitt is always careful to add, at least, that inner form is not didacticism, that he does not want literature to be "merely edifying."

Clearly, "inner form" is to the One as "outer form" is to the Many. Inner form is the permanent, the fixed, the insight in the poem; and outer form is the changing, the relative, the sensual aspect. Literary movements in his discussions are always contrasting currents which reflect his dualism: humanism as opposed to naturalism or neo-classicism as opposed to romanticism. Sometimes it is the lesser of two evils: a better phase of naturalism as opposed to a more vicious phase. In every case, moreover, his evaluation depends on the contrast at that particular point in the discourse. For example, he frequently compares nineteenth-century romanticism to eigh-

teenth-century classicism, and when he does, he favors the
eighteenth century. At another time, however, he may compare
neo-classicism with ancient classicism, and, in this case, the
eighteenth century exhibits an undesirable "formalism" in contrast to "true" ancient classicism. At still another point, he may
find even in ancient Greece evidence of a healthy classicism and
an unhealthy naturalism.

The levels of experience idea also figures prominently. When
literature sinks to the animal level, the naturalistic, it is inferior, one-sided. When a work reveals an "abiding human
element," however, then the artist has his creative eye on the
desirable "human norm." He admits that this criterion is
elusive and difficult to apply, but he insists on its validity
nonetheless.

We come now to Babbitt's theory of the inner check, individual control, and I want first to look at the concept as it
appears in his general philosophy, and then see what form it
takes in his critical theory.

We have seen how Babbitt's dualism gave him good and
evil. Now to do good and avoid evil one must "work," that is,
exercise control over one's evil nature. The one thing that
causes all forms of "naturalism" is what he calls ethical pas-
sivity: lack of control. When men are ethically passive, they
lust for power, for knowledge, or for sensation. When they
begin to exercise control, however, when they begin to "work,"
then they put the brake on temperament and impulse, and
become "ethically efficient."

Most moralists agree that happiness is the final goal, and
Babbitt does too. In order to be happy, he says, a man should
exercise his will and control his desires. The real basis of his
objection to Rousseauism is "that it is found not to make for
the happiness of the individual." When men exercise their
will, then they can successfully escape the whole vicious

influence of naturalism. Happiness is the aim, and the way to achieve it is to exercise control. As Babbitt explains, "My chief interest, in short, is in the problem of the will" and its relation to conduct, because however life might mock the philosopher, "the problem of conduct" always remains.

When one asks, however, just how this control is to be imposed, and just what is to guide us in our "ethical" effort, a fatal weakness appears. His answer to these questions is vague, confused, and unsatisfactory. It has been said that Babbitt is some kind of intellectual mutation, differing radically from his highly individualistic American forebears, a curiously late manifestation of some early foreign type, or, if native stock at all, then related to the American Puritanism of Jonathan Edwards; but Babbitt's failure to provide a concrete guide for the individual will, his peculiar form of self reliance, brings him closer to the typical Emersonian view. Babbitt found himself in this dilemma, I think, because of certain incompatible interests. For one thing, he was so convinced of the individual's ability to find his *own* way that he even lined up with his arch-enemies, the naturalists, on this one pont:

> I am with the naturalists who have from the start been rejecting outer authority in favor of the immediate and experimental .... My humanism is in this sense not only positive and critical, but, what will be found to come to the same thing, individualistic .... The significant struggle is between the sound and the unsound idividualist.[2]

Here, then, is Babbitt's problem. He refuses to sink to the naturalistic level where he must rely on purely private judgment, and he refuses to live on the religious level with the oppressive authority of any revealed religion. Of course, he hopes to live on the human level, as an individualist, but in order to avoid what he considers moral anarchy, in order to retain some authority over the individual, he coins a phrase, signifying nothing, and argues that it is a "psychological fact," a part of "the immediate data of consciousness," a matter of "primordial perception," a faculty which may be immediately and intuitively perceieved—"the higher will." Babbitt maintains that the higher will is neither God nor man, but it is somehow both. Some of the Catholic priests look upon Babbitt's concept of "the higher will" as evidence of "natural religion": a non-Catholic receiving grace without even realizing it. This natural religion business would not please Babbitt, however, for he wanted his morality without benefit of clergy.

Babbitt appears to be so afraid that the human "conscience" and the ordinary will may become a part "of the flux," that he dreams up the higher will and gives it power over both reason and the ordinary will. It is a faculty that can act as a check on the individual, or at other times, as a perceptive power, for it enables one to understand the proper limits of desire. The higher will is, therefore, an intuitive power, superior to ordinary faculties, and able to control and guide them. And as further support for the higher will, Babbitt suggests that it reflects something of still another supernatural entity, "the unmoved mover."

Of course, Babbitt always claims that the law of measure is the guide for the will, but the law of measure only warns us to avoid extremes. The question still remains: how, exactly, does one avoid extremes? His favorite term, "decorum," is usually applied if a man abides by the law of measure and is, therefore, little more than a sign of approval. And here again Babbitt himself is not moderate. Several of his opponents charged that he did not exhibit decorum in his violent attacks on naturalism. He simply replies that we must not confuse real tolerance with pseudo-tolerance. One can *not* be tolerant, he insists, when first principles are involved: that is only being muddle-headed. But if he is so vehement in his own attack, and yet practices decorum, we must conclude that being decorous is really being Babbitt. It is true, also, that Babbitt refers frequently and with approval to Aristotle's *Nicomachean Ethics,* but one suspects that he sees only Babbitt in Aristotle. So we are back where we started, with an intemperate insistence on individual control, but nothing concrete to guide the ethical effort.

Although Babbitt would not admit it, he moved to what he calls the religious level of experience with his doctrine of the higher will. He admits that "psychological analysis when carried to a certain point, encounters, in other terms, the same questions as theology," but he does not seem to realize that what he calls an empirical fact, the higher will, is essentially a spiritual entity. This longing for religious control, coupled with his reluctance to accept it, makes Paul Elmer More throw up his hands and cry, "When I try to grasp what Mr. Babbitt means precisely by the supernatural, I am held at bay by his sweeping reluctance . . . to associate it with any kind of dogmatic or revealed religion." The insight which Babbitt claims for the higher will leaves More still asking: "insight into what?" More admits that Babbitt's argument is a perfect one, link by link, except at the end, where it seems to be attached to nothing. Babbitt seems to reach so high to get some authoritative check on the individual that he is left suspended in thin air with no visible means of support.

In Babbitt's literary criticism the doctrine of the "ethical imagination" is the artistic counterpart of the higher will, because it is the writer's ethical imagination that assures the work a proper inner form and his aesthetic sense that supplies the outer form. Of course, Babbitt always says that writers must be aesthetically as well as ethically perceptive, must have artistic skill as well as a humanistic soul, but there is no doubt that inner form is the more important. He always praises the works with a solid inner form, and attacks those he considers corrupt.

We run into the same sort of difficulty with the ethical imagination that we encountered with the higher will. If inner form is to be the most important aspect of good art, and if the ethical imagination is to act as a guide to the writer and a check on him—then we must ask: How is the control to be exercised, and just what is to guide the writer's ethical imagination? Here, as with the higher will, Babbitt's answer is in one sense, unsatisfactory. The ethical imagination is definitely in "the realm of insight . . . [and] anterior to formulas." Since insight itself is superior to both thought and feeling, we have again a supernatural control over the writer's thoughts and feelings. As a further guide to the artist, Babbitt offers his own particular doctrine of "imitation." Inner form requires imaginative "allegiance to some central norm or scale of values . . . set above any particular art." "Inner form requires the conscious imitation of a model," but the model is not a worldly one. It is rather, a "supersensuous model," an "abiding human element" which can never be revealed by any dogma or creed, is not subject to rules, and can never be locked up in any formulas. Of course, Babbitt praises Shakespeare, among others, for dwelling close to the center of human nature, and some of the literature of ancient Greece also exhibits a perceptive and disciplined imagination. His theory, however, remains obscure. Babbitt leaves it up to a writer's supernatural ethical imagination to guide him to a proper imitation of a supersensuous model in order to create a work dealing with an abiding human element which can never be stated in words. Actually, the artist gets a blank check.

The objection is not that Babbitt's critical theory grants the artist considerable freedom; most theories do. The difficulty arises only because he himself places so much weight on *control* of the artistic imagination, the emotions, the thoughts. Even such critical terms as "the sublime," for example, become, in his vocabulary, indications of artistic control; "The sublime requires a curb or *frein vital.*" He constantly insists that any divorce of literature from ethical reality will deprive the work of the essential ethical element and, what is worse, free a lively aesthetic sense which is not then subordinate to any control by the ethical imagination. The imagination thus freed is apt to wander wild in a land of chimeras, and to dwell on the changing rather than the permanent. Yet, with all his emphasis on control, he offers in literature, as in life, no specific guide lines. If the ethical imagination is to offer insight, we might well ask as More did, "Insight into what?" And the law of measure will not help any more than it did before. His general ethical beliefs and his critical principles are indeed the same. You can separate the two, as we have here, but there is no real difference.

The Practice

There are some important differences between Babbitt's critical theory and his practice. If in his theory he pays his respects to what are called the aesthetic features of the art, in practice he hardly notices those aspects of the work. If in theory he feels that a critic should deal with all forms of literary expression, in practice he condemns any move in that direction. If his theory leaves the artist very little control outside himself, his practice more than makes up the difference, because Babbitt is a personified outer check on recognized masters and whole literary periods. As Arthur Lovejoy says, Babbitt "has attained the distinction of having damned a larger number of eminent and long accepted writers than any other modern critic." In short, if Babbitt's theory is broad and general, his practice is narrow and specific.

These characteristics, and others, too, appear in his estimate of fellow critics. There is, apparently, very little in the whole history of English criticism which pleases him. The criticism of the nineteenth century he sums up in one verbal snarl: "relativity." He charges romantic impressionist critics with losing self-control and using literature to give way to a "temperamental urge, to the uttering of one's gustos and disgustos." Saintsbury is one who confuses appreciation with judgment, and so forgets the prime function of criticism: evaluation. Saintsbury combines learning and romantic gusto, and his critical practice simply encourages others to fall into the moral anarchy of impressionism.

Babbitt is also suspicious of any non-humanistic literary scholarship. He points out, for instance, that Victor Cousin let his love for his field so override his sense of proportion, that he fell into the evil of what Babbitt calls "frenzied research for its own sake." Most often, however, Babbitt attacks critics for their failure to mirror his master ideas. Taine, for one, is less the critic because he does not believe in the inner check; both Sainte-Beuve and Edmond Scherer, while they have certain humanistic tendencies, nevertheless have too much naturalistic rot in their philosophies. Their humanism is too much a matter of taste, too individualistic. Madame de Staël holds to a vicious philosophy which acknowledges impulse to be a virtue. She does not realize that impulse has to be controlled. It is clear from these instances that when Babbitt evaluates critics, he measures them rather strictly, and strictly by his own brand of Neo-Humanism.

He does much the same sort of thing when he evaluates the more creative writers. Since Babbitt's dualism is one of his fundamental ethical principles, he defends it against all

61

attack. Just how important he considers the concept may be illustrated by his observation that if Frederick Schiller had solved the problem of dualism he would have been one of the great sages of all time. Babbitt believes that man is *both good and evil*, and any variation from the principle vitiates a writer's work. Since Babbitt himself put such great faith in the individual, it is not surprising that he contends that the American Puritan, Edwards, was wrong in thinking that man was *all* evil; but Emerson, on the other hand, errs in the opposite direction, because he erases sin by refusing to recognize the evil in human nature. While Babbitt praises M. Brunetière for attacking the doctrine of natural goodness, he blames Taine for weakening the belief in dualism, the best defense against moral chaos.

And Babbitt is quick to censure any writer who holds to what he calls a "false dualism." Rousseau, for instance, sets up a false dualism of the naturally good person opposed by a corrupt society. Babbitt feels that this view tends to shift moral responsibility away from the individual, where it belongs, and to place the blame on society. Poverty does not excuse the crime. In fact, he is suspicious of all literature which aims at economic reform. Socially conscious writers of plays, poems, and novels—all preach a false dualism which underplays individual responsibility. All reform must start and end with the individual.

Any denial of dualism is a threat to his notion of control, but any denial of free will is an even more ominous danger. When he looks at the early writing of George Sand, for instance, he thinks it bad; but when she finally becomes disillusioned with socialism and recognizes the truth of dualism and the power of the free will, then he praises her for finally accepting the moral law. It is a late repentance, Babbitt admits, but it comes in time to assure her a place among the great. In other words, Babbitt has no use for George Sand till she exhibits a view like his own, and the judgment really has very little to do with her work, because most of the evidence of her late humanism is in her letters rather than in her novels.

It is partly for the purpose of protecting his doctrine of free will that Babbitt attacks the literary movements known as "realism" and "naturalism." Theodore Dreiser's *An American Tragedy,* for example, does not rest on a belief in free will. For that reason, a reader can not derive from it the enlargement of spirit and relief which he should gain from true tragedy. Or Diderot's dramatic theory that man is determined entirely by environment leaves no room for the individual will, and so eliminates the "true drama" of "moral choice." When Taine develops the theory that man is determined by a combination of race and environment, he tosses man into the ebb and flow of natural forces. True naturalistic literature, moreover, does not rise above the ugly natural level of experience; hence it leaves one with a sense of utter futility and frustration. When the novelist Balzac depicts only the natural level of experience, only the brutal law of force pevails; and, Babbitt argues, since much more than brute force does exist in the world, then the picture of life in naturalistic literature is simply untrue. Realism is somewhat less reprehensible, but even realism can be carried so far that it too denies dualism and free will. At best, realism is a step in that direction.

In Babbitt's eyes, moreover, the whole romantic movement encourages moral laxness. The romantics deny the evil in man, they favor giving way to impulse, and they encourage us to sink to the level of the senses. They carefully avoid responsible action, by living in a world of illusion for the sake of illusion. The romantic is interested in art only as it relates to the senses, not as it appeals to the intellect and the will. Poetry becomes for the romantic a kind of lotus-eating with no rational or dramatic purpose: mere word painting—mere technique.

Babbitt's discussion of Wordsworth's poems is probably one of the best illustrations of how his literary dualism, the distinction between inner and outer form, encourages him to cut the helpless poem in two. Babbitt seldom gets the parts together again for any sort of rounded estimate.

It is true that Babbitt admits on occasion that the outer form of Wordsworth's poems is quite good. He even says once that Wordsworth is poetically most admirable when he is most dubious as a thinker. But Babbitt's judgments are ordinarily based entirely on the poem's inner form; and all Wordworth's poetry is vitiated finally because the poet confuses pantheistic reveries with genuine spiritual experience. In fact, Wordsworth so emphasizes pantheistic feelings rather than action, that he is a failure even as a narrative poet.

The following few lines from Browning will serve admirably to show how Babbitt pounces on the kind of nature poems typical of romanticism:

> Oh World as God has made it,
>   All is beauty
> And knowing this is love, and
>   Love is duty.

It seems to follow from these verses of Browning, perhaps the most flaccid spiritually in the English language, that to go out and mix one's self up with the landscape is the same as doing one's duty.[3]

Babbitt always regards such poetry as a subtle attempt to put forth as profound philosophy what is really a holiday view of existence. Needless to say, Babbitt never takes a holiday. There is "work" to be done, ethical work, seven days a week.

Ordinarily Babbitt does not make anything like a detailed analysis of a poem to substantiate his points, but on at least two occasions he does explicate *in extenso* with Browning's

The Ring and the Book, and Coleridge's *The Ancient Mariner.*
Since both these explications are interesting samples of his
practical criticism, I want to look at them briefly.

Babbitt says of *The Ring and the Book* that it lacks outer
form because of defective poetical technique, but he does not
make clear just what he means. He is chiefly concerned with
the ethical values in the poem. He thinks that Browning failed
to achieve inner form because he attempted to give a semblance
of seriousness to what was drastically unethical. The poem,
therefore, actually raises a prejudice against everything that is
"central." Decorous Guido is unattractive, while indecorous
Caponsacchi, the least representative of priests, is presented
sympathetically. Browning offers the value of physical love as
a substitute for both religion and philosophy and deliberately
sacrifices all ethical values to the beautiful moment, the *Sum-
mum Bonum.* All this leads Babbitt to the conclusion that there
is no such thing as "romantic morality."

When he inquires into *The Ancient Mariner,* he finds the
psychology, incidents, and setting disturbingly *marvelous* rather
than *real,* and hence not relevant to normal experience. He
feels that there is no action, and hence no unity of action. There
is only unity of feeling, and this shifts one's interest away from
action to mere emotion. The poem is inferior, therefore, because it is not properly concerned with moral choices and their
bearing on human happiness. It is impossible, he concludes, to
extract any serious ethical purport from the work. Babbitt
realizes, however, that the poem has a moral: the love of
humanity; but that kind of moral is a sham, and the poem thus
lays claim to a religious seriousness which it does not possess.
The Ancient Mariner, he believes, tries to stress subrationally
what is the equivalent of Christian charity.

In neither of these explications does Babbitt deal adequately with poetic technique, but his remarks on the inner form of

both poems do illustrate both his strength and weakness as a critic. A critic might well examine the ethical values, both explicit and implicit, in Browning's poem, but Babbitt's lament that decorous Guido is unattractive is only a crude stab in that direction. I cannot sympathize either with his desire to label Guido decorous, or Caponsacchi the least representative of priests. Browning here, as always, dealt with moral problems, and to maintain flatly that Browning raises a prejudice against everything "central" is merely to damn the poem—not to clarify the ethical or poetic issues. Only one thing is clear—Babbitt does not like the poem.

In his remarks on *The Ancient Mariner* Babbitt is probably at his worst. His broad and seemingly liberal principle that literature should deal with a "human norm" in this case becomes a blunt instrument which he uses to beat down a serious poetic fantasy. Babbitt's antipathy to the theme of the poem is typical of his frequently unreasonable and violent reactions to anything he thinks is "humanitarian." By a prodigious stretch of the law of cause and effect, he feels that any expression of sympathy for humanity denies the necessity of more individual control, opens the floodgates to socialism, and is, therefore, a long step in the wrong direction. Compassion, brotherly love, is somehow associated in his mind with socialism, and socialism is a specious mask for the envy of riches. He even refuses to admit that Christ advocated brotherly love, and he attacks Renan's *Vie de Jesus,* because he thinks Renan makes Christ's doctrine over into a series of sentimental humanitarian effusions, and thus sacrifices the true "masculine" religion of the will to a soft, "feminine" religion of the heart.

I want, finally, to draw attention to a few of the more interesting and valid critical principles which are scattered throughout Babbitt's works. They are usually stated in general terms and with very little concrete illustration, and he uses them often to bludgeon some despised "ism" rather than to elucidate. One such principle appears in *The New Laokoön*, a comparatively early book (1910), and, if he had held to this theory, he might have avoided the rigid separation he later made between inner and outer form. Babbitt suggests that the discipline required for inner form may be similar to that required for outer form. Modern poetry, he goes on, does not display form because the philosophy and the verse have become "shapeless" and the poems pure impressionism.

Again, in *Rousseau and Romanticism,* there are valuable critical ideas brought up, but for the most part undeveloped. Yvor Winters, as we shall see, adopts some of them and uses them for explication and evaluation of modern poetry. Paul Elmer More, too, makes significant use of one or two notions quite similar to these best features of Babbitt's criticism. Babbitt maintains, for instance, that the modern intoxication with novelty of subject and vocabulary, combined with the concentration on intense private feelings, has led to certain major poetic faults. Often the poetic symbol of the emotion, he feels, is pushed to the point of hallucination, so that there remains only the most tenuous connection between the writer and the thing symbolized. He points out that the romantic writer often dwells on what is unique for him alone rather than on what he has in common with other men, so that his symbols became unintelligible. Babbitt suggests also that "the disproportion between the outer incident" which occasions the poem and the poet's emotion as expressed in the work is often so great that the poem is just ludicrous. Of course, he abhors free verse, but he attacks it as a sign of formlessness in the artist and not specifically as poetic formlessness. He warns against the poetic use of nature as a mirror for the writer's mood, but he does not show why that hurts the value of the poem. He argues also that imagism, or a use of descriptive details for their own sake, seriously limits the poet's range. Lastly, his concept of romantic irony or self-mockery is an interesting critical principle, and in Winters's hands this too becomes an important tool for analysis and judgment. Babbitt, however, sees self-mockery mainly as a lack of decorum and an escape from tradition.

Having now examined Babbitt's critical theory and practice, we can draw together some of the main threads of the argument. Babbitt's literary criticism is marred by long discussions of socialism, education, President Wilson, labor unions, Christian Science, or woman's suffrage. In his chapter on romantic irony in *Rousseau and Romanticism,* for instance, he goes sailing away from the literary subject to comment on "paradox," the "idea of the infinite," the "perils of aimlessness," dreams, disillusion, and finally, irony. When he reviews S. P. Sherman's book on Matthew Arnold, he slights both Sherman and Arnold to launch into a discussion of the general issues raised by Arnold's philosophy. At times the connection between the literary problem at hand and the digression is stretched so thin that even Babbitt apologizes. After a long discussion of what he calls "modern sinking" (in the middle of his remarks on Schiller), he says, "I am, however, digressing from Schiller who is only remotely responsible, if at all, for the proficiency we have attained in the art of sinking!"

In general, Babbitt does not follow his own theory. Despite his broad principles, he is narrow and narrow-minded. He separates the philosophy and the artistic features of a work, pays homage to both, and then promptly forgets the outer form. When he does approach the work, he mechanically measures it by his dualism and doctrine of control. His understanding of individual control is a valuable, if limited, notion, but in his eyes everything is a threat to it: a simple nature poem, a love poem, an expression of sympathy for the poor or love for humanity. He finds "sham religion" or a viciously sentimental note in the most inoffensive verse. And all modern literature is just as offensive as all modern society. His few specific references to any modern work are usually only hasty condemnations. So much is bad that there is no real discrimination.

All these critical practices led Arthur Lovejoy to complain that Babbitt does not "consider the total character of the opinions or aesthetic qualities of the writers." Lovejoy thinks that as a critic Babbitt is "censorious and unimaginative" and wrote "primarily as a moralist." Even More, Babbitt's comrade-in-arms, says of Babbitt's work that "literature was one of the fields in which he exercised his dialectic."

Babbitt was himself aware of this failing. He constantly warns, "My treatment of certain eminent persons of the past and present . . . is limited by my subject, and makes no claim to completeness." On the question of whether he is basically a moralist, Babbitt is no less clear and positive. Speaking of his whole series of books, he says, "The volumes of the series are yet bound together by their common preoccupation with the naturalistic trend," and, as we have seen, naturalism is his synonym for evil. Acting as a philosopher-critic of his own special type, he was in his own eyes tracing "main currents as a part of . . . [his] search for principles to oppose to naturalism." And if we take Babbitt at his own word, he saw only certain sides of the writers and their work, but that never prevented him from making evaluations—and, therefore, curiously limited evaluations.

It is not easy to capture Babbitt or his criticism in any neat evaluation. He had amazing knowledge of literature, and unusual power to suggest how it might relate to the general life. But he was so much a moralist, so much the master rhetorican, that he was less effective as a critic. He wanted society to accept his master ideas before it was too late, and literature was only incidental to that end.

CHAPTER IV

Paul Elmer More

Babbitt and More are usually lumped together in accounts of American criticism, and in some ways they do belong together. They are both passionately devoted to the moral evaluation of literature; they share the same basic philosophy; yet there are significant differences between the two in both critical theory and practice.

If we turn now to More's work we can see just what those differences are, and, more important, we will find that More raises some aspects of the moral measure of literature that Babbitt never dreamed of.

Although Babbitt and More were life-long friends, and fought for humanism side by side, their views are so divergent that they really debated in a friendly fashion whenever they got together. It began when they first met in a Harvard graduate class. One gathers from More's description of that early encounter that he was a little appalled and overwhelmed by Babbitt, because he concluded that Babbitt was probably born with a full grown philosophy. Even as a young man, Babbitt confronted him with a complete view of life, and some twenty-five years later, when they were together again at Harvard, More noticed that Babbitt's ideas had not changed at all, except that they were "now reinforced by an appalling mass of erudition." Indeed, it is no wonder that More was amazed at Babbitt's consistent and solid views, because compared to Babbitt,

More was an intellectual chameleon. In the autobiographical *Pages from an Oxford Diary,* More explains that in the course of his life he had ranged all the way from romantic to sceptic, and from a semi-Eastern mystic to an orthodox Christian.

One of the most obvious points of difference between them, then, is that More needed the supernatural. While Babbitt shied away from revelation, More longed for religious guidance and found solace and comfort in submission to God. Once when they argued over the question of the significance of the supernatural, Babbitt ended the discussion by turning to More in exasperation and crying, "Good God, man, are you a Jesuit in disguise?" With a typical hesitancy More confessed, years later, that he had "never been able to answer the question satisfactorily."

The differences we find between Babbitt and More, both intellectual and religious, are probably rooted in differences of temperament and personality. As Sherlock Gass suggests, in *The Criers of the Shop:*

> Even after all ambiguity is cleared away, and literature
> . . . proves objectively to deal with a moral substance,
> temperamental differences will still tend to divide the
> lovers of literature at this point, some finding the values
> they seek in one variety of their responses, and some in
> another, and both passionate, since the sanction of their
> values is in their indisputable feelings.[1]

The Theory

More's acceptance of an ever present supernatural power affects his dualism and, of course, his ethics. As early as 1894, in the semi-autobiographical work, *The Great Refusal,* he reveals a deep longing for reality beyond this realm. The hero of that fragmentary and sentimental novel tries to find "celestial beauty" in an earthly love affair, but his infinite longings are unsatisfied by mundane love and later develop into the infinite doubts of romantic scepticism. He is finally saved from this state by an "inner voice" which helps him discover a "mystic haven of rest." And when his worldly passion completely "evaporates into clouds of mysticism," when he can no longer find peace in any of the common faiths, he turns, like More himself, to the Indian Brahma for relief.

While More did not remain a Brahman mystic for very long, he was nevertheless always impressed by what he calls the essential mystery of the universe, and he never tries to support it with anything but blind faith. He accepts dualism, for example, an an "irrational fact" and makes no attempt to argue that it is a verifiable psychological truth. The distinction between man's power of control and his impulses, between the calm and the flux, between good and evil, is for him "an irrational paradox rooted in the nature of things." It is an irrational axiom that "stands out more clearly the more it is questioned."

To be sure, the mature More never directly experiences the supernatural. So far as I know, he never disappears all the way into an undifferentiated Asian continuum, but he is perfectly content with intuitive perception as the basis for his belief in dualism. He even argues that intuition enables one to come closer to the truth than any reasoning process, and he believes that it is the same as the "faculty of religious insight wherever and whenever this" is to be found; and the "vital truth" of religion is the "bare consciouness of a dual tendency in human nature." His dualism, then, is central to his philosophy and to his religion. The moral quality of an individual or of a nation is directly proportional to a concern with *The One* rather than *The Many,* and any attempt to deny the relevance of this final test weakens the very sinews of morality, and tends to reduce man to a state of moral indifference. As might be expected, More attacks the evil of naturalism mainly because it tends to deny "revealed authority and supernatural intuition."

Since More so freely and without apology accepts an irrational way of knowing, he objects to Babbitt's suspicion of revelation and religion. More feels that humanism without religion lacks purpose, that the humanist needs faith to keep from sinking to the level of naturalism; and, most important for literature, "whenever great art has flourished, noble in theme as well as technique, there religion . . . has been present in the background," coloring the thoughts and emotions of men and supplying the everyday world with the "glamour of the supernatural."

More's doctrine of individual control is also influenced by his belief in the supernatural. The natural faculty of reason, he says, can not control impulse, for reason itself is apt to be part of the flux. Only intuitive insight can clearly perceive the constantly indwelling spirit of control—the inner check—and help one avoid the vice of extremes. An individual's morality is, therefore, "determined by the exercise or the quiescence of the inner check." Thus, the human level of experience is not nearly enough for More, and as he grows older his God ages along with him, changing from the rather indistinct spirit of his early romantic period, to a stern old Jehovah whose sharp commands are usually: "Thou Shalt Not." In short, the One is God, and the inner check is His power, and great art will somehow reflect those eternal truths.

Paul Elmer More certainly would agree with Babbitt, however, that the problems of literature and society are essentially the same; but, compared to Babbitt, More deals with those problems as they appear in literature rather than in society. Eleven of the fourteen volumes of his *Shelburne Essays*, for instance, are exclusively devoted to literature. When More does see confusion in literature, he calls it a consequence of "a similar confusion in our ideas," for "as we live, so shall we paint and write." If there is formlessness and a loss of higher emotion in letters, then we can find the "same thing in society." The critic, in his scheme, is the very one who must recognize the link between literature and life. The critic must act as a restraining influence to prevent excess in literature, he must set the literary canons, and he must act the part of a personified literary check.

The true critical spirit, moreover, will help us get at "the heart of things and strip the good from the bad," so the critic's primary function is moral evaluation. In the preface to the *Shelburne Essays VIII*, More defends himself against the objection that he stretches writers "on the rack of a harsh ethical formula" by saying that, while there is certainly a place for the sympathetic criticism of "appreciation," there is an even greater need to examine the ethical implications of a work. More says that no criticism should follow either mode exclusively, and he contends that he tries to maintain a moderate position between the two by pointing to merits in the work, and also to its ethical influence. But when a critic sees values in the art which he feels will lead to the dissolution of all he holds dear, then he must look to the influence on society. More declares that while writers like Browning or Tolstoy arouse his impatience because they claim to be spiritual leaders, others, like Sterne or Walpole, have no such pretensions and are simply entertainers. A critic, then, may have to take a stand on fundamental questions when he discusses Browning, but he can review Sterne with only mild appreciation of the merits. If the work contains great moral wisdom, however, then the critic must help the reader see its "ethical interpretation of individual and social experience, not only as these ideas are expressed directly and didactically, but more particularly in that glancing and suggestive manner which Matthew Arnold meant to convey in his phrase, 'the criticism of life'." The critic should make clear just how the work has "value as a literary discipline containing an imperishable criticism of life."

While More has the same sort of moral earnestness as Babbitt, still he is very much aware of Babbitt's worst critical faults. He understands how critical dualism encourages Babbitt to butcher poetry by cutting it into inner and outer form. He admits that Babbitt merely glanced at the inner form before he turned to the general moral problem. To avoid these difficulties himself, More developed several theories, based on his ethics, which he hoped would link the good and the beautiful and allow him to account for the aesthetic aspects of a poem as well as all the rest. In a word, he wanted critical principles which would make the *whole poem* subject to moral evaluation.

First, we will see how More separated the two aspects of a poem, and then how he tried to relate them to his ethics. He employs the familiar distinction between "form" and "content." Using aesthetic standards alone, one can not measure the greatness of literature, but one can determine whether the work is *art* only by aesthetic principles. The best poem is one with a noble content expressed in perfect images, rhythm, and sounds.

If the artist's excellence is a function of his belief in dualism and his exercise of individual control, then More has a chance to show how these characteristics can affect the form and content of the art; and, in general, More insists that the ethical quality of the poet and the moral quality of his work are so closely related that to examine a writer's life is to criticize his poems. Indeed, he seldom tries to separate the two, and he always includes a biographical sketch of the artist in his essays. He is not always successful, however, in his attempt to integrate the life and the work, for they are often unrelated sections of a single essay. And he seems, at times, to confuse his admiration for the writer *as a man* with the author's worth *as an artist*. In his essay on Charles Lamb, for instance, he says, "It is the man Charles Lamb, after all, which makes his writings so precious."

But even if he is not always successful, it is still important to note just how More tries to relate the artist and the work. One of his suggestions is that a writer's philosophy affects both the form and content of his work. In both his life and work, for example, Walter Pater displays an evil and insinuating interest in hedonism. Moreover, the Victorian "philosophy of change" affects both the style and the substance of the verse of that era, with the harmful effects of the philosophy appearing in the very rhythms. On another occasion he observes that William Morris's "sense of moral values is of the most rudimentary sort." One can have, therefore, little "human sympathy with his characters" in *Sigurd The Volsung*. Even the mood and texture of Morris's verse is "inhuman and elfin."

More maintains, also, that a writer's belief in dualism affects the form of his poetry, for somehow a poet displays dualism in the language itself. Heine's poem, *Du Bist Wie Eine Blume,* exhibits an "enigmatic dualism," "a sense of transiency that runs through the heart of the world." Longfellow's poems, however, do not have this desirable dualism. More confesses that this standard is difficult to apply, but he argues that it goes to the root of good criticism. When he discusses the work of William Butler Yeats, he contends that the poet has mentally drifted off into a hazy dreamland of vague sorrow and reverie which is revealed "unmistakably in a curious uncertainty of rhythm, wherein the accents hover weakly and dissolve into a fluttering movement utterly different" from the sure, strong rhythms of the best poets. More asserts that Anatole France has a "philosophy of life" which is "tainted with moral indolence, which betrays itself in his literary productions and to some extent in his critical standards."

Another way More tries to link the poet with his work is to show that the poet's spirit, or "temperament," affects both the paraphrasable content and the style. As he explains, "The temperament of the writer dominates his work to so overmastering a degree that to unfold the one is properly to criticize the other." Hazlitt, for instance, has the "untamed passion of the revolutionary spirit," and it accounts for the "singular unevenness of his work." It can be seen in his language, in both the keenness and the limits of his psychological insight and in the many contradictions in his beliefs, and it accounts also for his "rapid style." Hazlitt's whole life is a "wayward career;" he lived in an "irregular way," and those characteristics are unmistakable in all his work. In More's opinion, when John Donne breaks with the conventional poetic technique and poetic language of his day, he exhibits "the whim and license of the impertinent individual." With this critical principle, More often uses such terms as "impertinent" in poetic technique. Milton, for example, is so impertinent that he develops into an undisciplined political radical. More does admire *Lycidas* intensely, but he explains that it was written before Milton's longing for liberty turned into a desire for "license." More claims that the style of Milton's prose tracts is very faulty, and he insists that the "poor style" of the political writings has "a close relation to the fact that when he passes from imagination to [political] theory his voice is not that of his people, but of an exasperated individual." It is unfortunate that More does not pursue this line of analysis into the really difficult problems of Milton's writing. For example, he does not attempt to show how Milton's prose style in the essay on education differs from the style found in the essay on regicide. The former, I assume, can hardly be considered the voice of an exasperated individual;

the latter, however, must have disturbed More. And More never discusses the anti-Papist sonnet, *On The Late Massacres in Piedmont,* with this critical standard in mind.

A third way More has of relating the moral quality of the artist and his work is his theory that what he calls the psychological adjustment of the writer is reflected in the art. How does the artist achieve this state of balance? By exercising his power of control. If he has an active inner check, then he will enjoy the proper mental balance, an inner harmony, and it will be reflected in the beauty of his writing. More maintains, for example, that Kipling fails to see that beauty in literature is the "expression of an inner harmony of the faculties depending on the . . . will to refrain." It is the law of measure *"nothing too much* working itself out in perfect proportion of thought and form." More says that Longfellow has no "inward check," no inner harmony of faculties. As a consequence his verses flow "too smoothly and fluently." His work is not steeped in the "deeper and more obstinate emotions of the breast." Dickens, too, in More's eyes, never learned "resignation and discipline" from his days of poverty; he does not have the "aristocratic element [which] denotes self-control, discipline, suppression" in either his character or his art. Dickens lacks perfect form and morality in his books, because the absence of restraint passes "as how could it help passing, into his work." If Dickens himself has no "measure of voluntary self-discipline," then he can not create a character who has the quality of a true gentleman.

More's remarks on Dickens, in this passage and in others, provide a striking example of one of his less attractive and constantly recurring attitudes. Dickens was, in More's eyes, a man from the lower classes who merely pretended to literary eminence. One might expect literary ability to appear in the upper classes, but not in the lower depths. I am reminded that

78

E. M. Forster says that he gets the impression from the criticism of T. S. Eliot "that the Muses are connected not so much with Apollo as with the oldest county families," and More leaves the same impressioon.

In these three ways, then, More hopes to relate the moral quality of the writer with the excellence of his art, and, in each case, either the ideas of the artist or his power of control is crucial, but More also refers to an impersonal restraint on the artist that is inherent in the literary form or in the subject and is quite independent of the author. For example, More argues that when Whitman breaks from the poetic convention of exact rhythm, he cuts himself off from a desirable kind of restraint which grows out of the demands of human nature. The difficulties of form, he contends, occasionally impose enough of a check on Longfellow so that his rhymed poems are better than his blank verse; but he is not at his best in the more elaborate and restrictive sonnet forms. More also seems to think that the meaning itself can impose a restraint on the verse, for he characterizes Swinburne's *Dolores* as a poem in which "the thought has no sure control over the words." Emerson's poems often betray a looseness and formless spontaneity of style. When, on the contrary, Emerson turns to the subject of restraint, his language becomes instantly terse, and falls naturally into symmetrical form. More never fully explains this principle, and it does not often appear, so it is really only a shadowy suggestion; but it does raise the possibility of the meaning itself determining poetic form.

In drama, too, More feels the form can act as a restraining influence. When the Elizabethan dramatists try for an "exquisite fancy" for which the first "impulse of genius" is sufficient, when they portray a violent passion in a drama "whose looseness of structure imposes no restraint," then they can bring forth fresh dramatic beauty; but "put on them the habit

79

of a stricter art, bid them confine their expression to a mould where form and conscious style are essential," and they are less successful. Under such restraint their sentiment becomes "frigid and unreal."

And a final instance of More's theory that the form itself can check the writer is his idea that the use of symbols is a dangerous thing, because it fails to provide the proper restraint. He objects that symbols can entice an artist like William Sharp away from the real world of moral responsibility, and lead him into an imagined realm which is "more and more fantastically unreal." When Proust employs symbols, he drifts off into "symbolism" and so eliminates the "faculty of responsible selection." Symbols are also an attractive technique for the emotional pantheist, because the pantheist vaguely suggests that something in the natural world is a symbol of his intense feelings, but he never really explains what evokes his emotions. More notices in Edgar Allan Poe this same "dissolution of the solid world of phenomena into images of an inner fluctuation of the soul which is the very essence of 'symbolism'." And he admires the fact that Crabbe carefully distinguishes between man and nature and never blends them into a "haze of symbolism."

In all these instances, there is the strong suggestion that symbols overstimulate the imagination and encourage one to escape from the world of moral responsibility. Although More never states it in just such terms, part of his objection seems to be that symbols do make for obscurity in literature. His notion that the symbolic technique of the pantheist provides no clear motivation for the poet's feeling, for instance, calls attention to obscure motivation in lyric poetry. Winters, as we shall see, makes good use of this argument in his analysis of obscurity in modern verse.

There is ample evidence to indicate that More feels that he successfully linked the aesthetic qualities of literature to the ethical principles, but he does little more than assert the relation. He fails to explain, with analysis of the form, just how the rhythm shows a "looseness" or an "unevenness," a "radical spirit" or a "wayward career." He touches on the possibility, and then leaves the details to the reader. Neither does he bother to support the interesting notion that the poetic or dramatic form can provide a check; he merely states it. Even in an essay devoted to English verse forms, he does not show how the form itself might be a restraining influence. There is, then, nothing like a modern close reading or detailed attention to the text. When More does comment directly on such matters as rhythm or style, he expresses himself figuratively. While we may *feel* the effectiveness of the poetic form, he says, we can not adequately describe it, and close analysis is simply not helpful. It is typical of More's method, therefore, to quote a bit of verse he likes, and then glide away from it, blowing adjectival kisses and cooing that it has a certain "indefinable charm," a "swinging melody," a "sweetness," a "clear, unearthly loveliness," or the "slender brittleness of a costly vase." More can point to an occasional unlicensed blemish in Keats's poems, to the "thinness" of Tennyson's style, or suggest that Whittier needs a "purely literary canon" which would improve the quality of his verse; but beyond that kind of adjectival evaluation, he offers little evidence to support his judgments of either good or bad aesthetic features. Apparently he feels that careful analysis of the art is incompatible with aesthetic pleasure.

While More is much more conscious of the aesthetic features than Babbitt, he is at one with Babbitt on the proposition that the aesthetic charms of a work can never take the place of the "spiritual truth" necessary for great literature. English literature indeed is the best of all modern literature because of its "deep rooted conventions of moral responsibility," and ancient Greek literature owes its excellence to its fine ethical content. Like Babbitt, More often maintains that, while the literary artist is not to preach, still he should display the dual nature of man and the principle of control. We shall turn now to see in some detail how More employs those two ethical standards.

More's dualism is essentially a religious principle involving a distinction between the divine and the human, the Christian soul and the flesh. For that reason, More feels that dualism must underlie poems which appeal to our deepest sensibilities, and it can justly serve as a test of the highest artistic endeavor. More acknowledges that Wordsworth has beautiful flashes in his verses, and an admirable, agitated moral sense, but still Wordsworth's poetry is not of the highest order because he turns to an amoral nature, to the murmur of the evening wind, rather than to the still voice within to find a guide.

More reserves some of his harshest contempt, moreover, for writers who seem to deny that man is inherently evil—with the evil underlined. Emerson for one recognizes dualism too "jauntily," and since he fails to see the full significance of dualism, Emerson suffers from a serious "limitation of spiritual experience" which makes him indifferent to moral and personal responsibility. Browning also fails to recognize the dualism "of the lower and higher nature of man, or between the human and the celestial character." In More's eyes, Browning dresses a "worldly and easy philosophy in the forms of spiritual faith," and so deceives those who seek the higher truths in his verse. More points also to a fundamental inconsistency in Pope's verse. While Pope says that man is naturally good, he nevertheless finds it necessary (in the satires) to attack the evil in human nature with a rich vocabulary and violent wrath. Lastly, in More's eyes, Tennyson in some poems wrongly glosses over dualism in his willingness to compromise, but at times (in the Holy Grail poems, for instance) Tennyson is a "poet of insight" who properly distinguishes the eternal world from the material world. As these examples suggest, the religious dualism in More's hands is flexible enough to enable him to unearth the inconsistency between Pope's philosophy and his satire, as well as to admire some of Tennyson's religious poems. In other words, More can use the principle for an analysis of the ideas and also evaluation.

Probably the least admirable aspect of More's thinking, and it affects his literary judgments, is his complete contempt for any reform of society to equalize opportunity. As with Babbitt, so here, the only valid reform must begin and end with the individual. All other efforts at reform will either fail or destroy all that is good. He praises Thoreau, for instance, because the New Englander's reliance on the doctrine of control is so sturdy that it can not "be perturbed by the inequalities and sufferings of mankind," and Thoreau's faith in the individual is so strong that he has no humanitarian interest in the masses. And the word *humanitarian*, for More, is just an oath. He despises anyone who shows the slightest sympathy for the poor. Even the rather mild nineteenth-century English reformer, John Morley, First Viscount of Blackburn, has too much "sympathy for the less fortunate." Rousseau's false dualism of the good individual as opposed to the evil society is also a particularly bad "mechanical parallelism" which leads to such evils as Communism. When More discusses Tolstoy, he fairly rages at "the arrogant dogmatism of this Russian bigot." He hates Tolstoy's version of "the brotherhood of man," and he sees it as an appeal to men's emotions which will ultimately destroy all sound judgment. The whole tone of his remarks is bitter and violent. When a "red" humanitarian crosses his path, More abandons the literary problem, throws off his usual gentility, and goes into a rage. In an article on "Halifax," for instance, he indulges in a long attack on brotherly love which has no clear relation to the subject. A humanitarian brings out the worst in More, and the automatic reaction simply blinds him to any virtues in a writer who is critical of the social structure.

Like Babbitt, More also makes wide and varied use of the principle of individual control in his literary evaluations. The two master ideas of dualism and control, of course, are closely tied together, but it is still possible to see the great emphasis on control, for most literary evils spring from an author's failure of will. When one loses control, he is apt to show an "infinite craving," a "wild emotion," the "confusion of the sensuous and the spiritual," or the "glorification of temperament" in a wilful riot of expansive desires. Romanticism is a single word for all these vicious tendencies, and classicism, on the other side, is a synonym for moral health. The whole romantic movement is, in effect, an attack on judgment, decorum, and the law of measure. More distinguishes, however, between a "universal romanticism," which can be seen in moments of high poetic inspiration, the purest poetry of any age, and a vague reverie, which ends in the pantheism of Wordsworth and his school.

But More's attack on both Keats and Shelley is far from a wholesale condemnation. He thinks Shelley is at his finest as a lyric poet, but even there Shelley's poetry is marred occasionally by his tendency to exercise enthusiasm rather than the inner check. While Keats has a sense of eternal beauty which is a "partial glimpse" of the "reality," an "imperfect view," there is still "danger lurking in its fair deception," because the young poet is essentially undisciplined, and therefore remains "in a state of morbid fermentation."

In another essay More carefully distinguishes between Thoreau's love of nature and the nature poems of the English romantics. More likes Thoreau for the very reason that he has no revolutionary doctrine to mix up with the Alpine solitudes, and Thoreau has nothing of Keats's passionate and voluptuous self-abandonment. Thoreau is not like Shelley either, for his New England moral sinews would not tolerate the Englishman's mental dissipation. Thoreau's "reliance on the human will" is sturdy, and his "faith in the individual" unshaken. There is not a trace of "foreign pantheism" in Thoreau either, so his insight is true and wholesome. But despite these unflattering remarks about Shelley and Keats, More concludes his discussion of Thoreau by declaring that the American's creative ability is by no means equal to the genius of the two English poets. Now, this surprising turn of judgment, not infrequent in More, indicates that he does not always follow his own theories about the relation between the ethical and the aesthetic content of literature. Apparently More has a high regard for the romantic poets; yet he feels that he should attack their philosophies. But how can Keats and Shelley have such creative genius, and such bad ideas? Why doesn't Thoreau's insight make him rank above the English poets? The answer is clear enough. More simply forgets about the relation between the poet's beliefs and his style.

In much the same way, More relies on a standard of individual control in judging the Victorian writers. Perhaps most surprising is his estimate of Newman. Because of his own religious experience, one might expect More to warm up to Newman, and he does praise Newman's fight against the materialism of the age; but there is in Newman's religious conversion something of "failure in duty, a betrayal of the will."

He believes that Newman lost his vision of the true infinite and sought a substitute in the limitless expansion of emotions. Kipling's work, too, in More's opinion, suffers from too much emphasis on the will to act and too little on the will to refrain. When Kipling does not emphasize the will to refrain, he helps to open the way to sham spirituality and the "allurements of the senses," and the error is so grievous that it keeps him from the ranks of the great poets. Finally, as one might expect, Fitzgerald's *Rubáiyát* is for More the zenith of surrender to the senses, and the writing of William Sharp has such a debilitating effect on the will that to read him is be left a "helpless prey" to naturalistic forces.

Closely related to this narrow insistence on individual will is More's attitude toward women. He thinks that woman's suffrage will simply ruin the country, and he is convinced that one serious threat to twentieth-century society comes from Jane Addams's charity work in Chicago's Hull House. His antipathy to women social workers invalidates many of his judgments. He apparently thinks that women should be passive, acquiescient, and in no way pretend to a masculine, controlling will. I gather that he feels that women are all right so long as they stay in their places, but Mrs. Browning gets out of line and tries to affect a masculine will. She pretends to a strong character, and More protests the deception. When a woman has no intellectual pretensions, however, when she stays in her place *morally,* More is tolerant of her ethical and literary foibles to an astonishing degree. He takes considerable delight, for example, in the work of an obscure poetess, Louisa Shore, even though she has no particular philosophy, loves the illusions of elf-haunted gardens, believes in progress, and is an agnostic. Love can bring together contraries, but this affair between Paul and Louisa is an astonishing *non expectandum,* to coin a Latin phrase.

A Freudian could have a field day with More's attitude toward sexual details in literature. He is not so much blind to sex as he is supersensitive. He agrees, for instance, that sex is a fact of life, but one of those "brutal facts" that we ought to ignore as much as possible. Sexual desire is our animal side, and we must control it. Thus, an author should exercise control, and treat physical love as secondary. As More expresses it, the writer should look for the "sense of beauty that arises out of the brute fact, as a flower springs from the earth." He is to see the "ethical associations attached to love," because only in the solid reality of those associations, only in the eternal principles of right and wrong, can the artist find significant reality. Obviously the writer's will is involved in the way he treats the subject, so it is a weakness of will and an artistic fault when Balzac describes one of his heroines as the kind of girl who would appeal to a Parisian *roué*. More thinks that descriptions of women ought to be so chaste that they can not stimulate "physical disquiet." He argues that the nature of a young girl's attraction is sufficiently clear without any disturbing details, and he advocates, in effect, a law of measure for describing female characters. One of the few good things More has to say about Poe is that he does not explore sexual morbidity. When More discusses the decadent wits of the English 1890's, however, he accuses them of all the vices of sex, drink, and dope. He argues that a good author must necessarily create evil characters, but that we must hold the artist responsible for the "moral atmosphere" of his story. With this standard he damns Restoration comedy because it wallows in "nastiness." And moving from the decadent writing of Tieck to the writing of Thoreau is like passing "from a sick chamber to the breath of the fields." When he approaches the warm sensuousness of Swinburne, More goes wild with rage and hurls verbal thunderbolts: a "lack of emotional breeding," an "indecency," a

"hungering for forbidden fruit." Swinburne is best character-
ized, More concludes, by the word "satiety," the "most immoral
in the language," a word which will cause revulsion "in any
wholesome mind."

While it is certainly not unusual for critics to object to
Restoration comedy, or even to Swinburne on these grounds,
the remarkable feature of More's attack is its intensity. This
vehemence gets him into the characterization of Dostoyevsky's
Crime and Punishment as "filth, disease, morbid dreams,
bestiality, insanity, sodden crime," and he sees the same sort of
"filth" in Tolstoy and Strindberg. Even Galsworthy is guilty
of a "sickly analysis of illicit emotion," a "constant insinuation
that the only escape of the spirit from . . . stolid defeat is
through the passionate obsessions that cannot decently be
satisfied." And he finds Yeats's references to women's hair a
sign of a decadent "unwholesomeness."

It is difficult to separate More's antipathy for humanitarians from his dislike for "bestial" details in literature, because
socialism and sex seem to go together. Tolstoy is "unclean"
and "decadent" in his *Resurrection,* and a humanitarian social-
ist at the same time. Both qualities in Tolstoy so disturb More
that we get nothing near a literary judgment.

More also seems to believe that every day and in almost
every way literature is getting worse and worse, because he
soundly and completely damns almost all modern writing, and
he views the future with horror. When a work is pre-nineteenth
century, however, even he may excuse a little sex. More comments quietly on the sexual passages in Rabelais and Sterne:
"I can not see what harm can come to a mature mind from
either Rabelais or Sterne."

Perhaps More thought that only the best people read
Rabelais or Sterne. He is sure, however, that many people
read Dos Passos and James Joyce. And his blasts against all the

moderns (he seems to hate all but Edith Wharton, E. A. Robinson, and Robert Frost) are based largely on his dislike of the sexual details. James Branch Cabell's writings are, for More, "cunningly suggestive lubricity." Dreiser shows nothing of the higher side of life and Don Passos's *Manhattan Transfer* is "an explosion in a cesspool." Masters's *Spoon River Anthology* is "malodorous," and Sherwood Anderson's obsession with sex so overpowers the author that he is unable "to check the flood of animal suggestions" that issue from his bestial brain. More is almost pathetically and helplessly upset by "the moral slough of *Ulysses*." He realizes the *Ulysses* is not "haphazard writing," he knows that it is the product of a "brain busily engaged," and yet he feels that the work comes from that

> . . . dark region of the soul below the plain of ordered and rationalized life . . . . Rational selection and spiritual authority have been repudiated and the only law governing the flux is the so-called association of ideas, the fact that one image by some chance similarity evokes another and one sensation fades into another . . . . Sheer ugliness and morbid perversions abound in this stream [of consciousness] from the bottom of man's being.[2]

It is with "dismay and sadness," then, that More watches Joyce's genius disintegrate, and the artist expend his effort on "details of tumescent filth" which a normal mind can not "imagine and that it would be a pollution even to quote." In one sentence More condemns *Ulysses* as the ultimate in lust, violence, and blasphemy against the most high. Proust, besides being a symbolist, also concentrates on the ugly and bestial. Of course More has little regard for modern drama either, because "the insidious theory that associates art and spirituality with license and disease" has given us the revolting "nastiness of the stews" on the modern stage. In one of his most remarkable judgments, More claims that Shaw's drama *Fanny's First Play* attempts to show "that spirituality is the product of vice, and that the uniting bond of society is the revolt against restraint." I suppose this sort of evaluation can be understood only when one remembers that Shaw was a despised humanitarian social-ist, as well as the author of *Mrs. Warren's Profession*.

Thus, unlike Babbitt, More at least mentions many modern writers, but he damns the lot. Whenever he encounters modern "realists," he is anything but the judicious critic. He is, rather, so excited by the sex that he sees it everywhere, and it is all corruption and filth. He never tries to distinguish between justifiable sexual details (with both a moral and a literary pur-pose) and straight pornography. That failure turns him, at times, into an ignorant vice crusader.

Although More does not excuse the Elizabethan writers for their "excesses" in language, he is, in general, remarkably cool toward their plays. In order to understand this at all, we must notice how he applies his doctrine of control. For his Puritani-cal attack on the theater, *Histriomastix: The Player's Scourge or Actor's Tragedy* (1632), William Prynne earned in his own day the cruel sentence of the loss of both ears, the brand "S. L." (seditious libeller) on both cheeks, a fine of five thousand pounds, and life imprisonment. Since that time, Prynne has continued to attract the abuse of innumerable critics. More, too, regrets Prynne's failure to see any good in the plays, but when Prynne lashes out at the evil audiences of the time, More defends him:

> Prynne does . . . approach the real evil of the late Eliza-bethan drama. In saying that the audiences took delight in the representation of wickedness without sin-lamenting sorrow, he has merely changed into what we may be pleased to call religious cant, the fundamental literary criticism that these plays deal with the expression and interaction of passions in themselves with little sense of

character. For it must be observed that moral judgment and literary criticism go hand in hand. There is no doubt much to condemn in Beaumont and Fletcher from the direct standpoint of public decency; but, on the other hand, they are full also of moral sentiments magnificently expressed. The real moral indictment under which they lie is rather the more central charge that in ignoring that element of our being which stands apart from the passions as a governing power, they loosened the bond of character, removing from conduct the law of cause and effect and leaving human nature as a mere bundle of unrelated instincts. That is the moral judgment, and the aesthetic criticism is but the same thing in different words.[3]

In this passage about Elizabethan drama, More hints at the dire social consequences of the plays, but he ordinarily argues the case in strictly literary terms. He feels, for instance, that a play should display a unity of emotions and understanding. An audience may feel the emotions of the characters, but, More insists, we can understand only when we see the principle of unity at work in the internal struggle between passion and restraint. If the play portrays that struggle, then the audience can experience the highest aesthetic delight. The Puritans, he feels, restored a proper emphasis on the moral battle, and John Bunyan, while he oversimplifies, is still nearer the Greeks than he is to the Elizabethan dramatist, because Bunyan recognized the importance of control. Even if we admit More's criticism to be sound, still his admiration for Bunyan is strange, for, in *Pilgrim's Progress,* the inner struggle is translated into quite external and allegorical terms.

More is also disturbed that *Romeo and Juliet* does not contain an internal struggle. Altogether, the play fails because the tragedy is occasioned by such things as sexual desire and a family feud, rather than the inner struggle of true tragedy. In fact, More laments that the typical Elizabethan characters squander their passions rather than restrain them. Only Shakespeare in his greatest tragedies rises above the moral level of the age, and he ranks with the best of the ancient Greeks who understood that "tragic pity and horror are based on this distinction between passion and the inner citadel of character."

In his dramatic criticism, I would say, More is led into poor judgments by his doctrinaire insistence on the control of passion. *Romeo and Juliet* is not Shakespeare's best, but to complain that the lovers' emotion is sinful and that the tragedy has no real significance, is to carry the principle to an absurdity. And the observation that Bunyan is closer to Greek tragedy than many of the Elizabethans is a clear indication that something has gone wrong, for the drama of that particular period is remarkable for its depiction of inner conflict. It is perfectly correct for More to ask for inner conflict, but when his understanding of just what that means is so narrowed that he can not find it in Elizabethan drama, then his judgment is not reliable.

In his discussion of novels, More's principle of control is also important, because here too his notion of tragedy depends upon the "conflict in human motives between the universal and the particular, the changeless law and the temporal passion." When characters are not shown to be under the control of the will, as in some of George Meredith's works, no true characterization is possible. In the first period of his career, George Gissing has, according to More, a "profound sense of morality" and leaves the reader conscious of a "sense of personal responsibility," but in the second period he loses this quality, becomes sex conscious, "and with this change [there] comes a certain relaxing of moral fiber," and Gissing turns instead to humanitarian crusades. Finally, however, Gissing again wins More's approval, in a third period, when he shows no reforming zeal, and becomes instead an anti-democratic aristocrat. We should add that Gissing's final period is not very relevant to the literary discussion, for the novelist wrote no fiction during that time; but it is surprising that More likes him at all because Gissing's idol was the hated Charles Dickens.

In his discussions of the novel, More often says that he has very little use for writers who mechanically reinforce the morality by rewarding the good people and punishing the bad. He says such novels are little better than "Sunday School stories" and simply not true to life. The author should use indirect methods to suggest his own evaluation of the action. If the novelist remains completely indifferent, however, if he simply lets the facts of the story speak for themselves, then he runs the risk of separating the art from life by his own indifference. The novelist, in short, should have an ethical theory, but he "should screen his ethical theory under the guise of an objective presentation of life." However, on occasion, More certainly does not object to the artist clearly indicating his own feelings toward the characters, because he likes Trollope's method of explicitly taking the reader into the moral plan of the novel, and he praises Trollope for relentlessly following the consequences of "little defalcations of will."

While in theory More calls for an objective presentation of life, in practice he really wants the author's hints to be rather broad and intrusive. As in his dramatic criticism, More insists on individual responsibility in the novel, and it leads him to an extreme position. He is so unwilling to allow any emphasis on the influence of environment that he scorns novelists like Dickens, Tolstoy, Samuel Butler, Sinclair Lewis, and Joyce.

There are, finally, two features of More's criticism which can best be illustrated by looking at typical essays. First, it should be clear that More does occasionally leave his literary subject far behind and go off on a tirade against modern education, politics, crime, Christian Science, woman's suffrage, or the "ugly" foreign influence in our cities. In an article on Huxley in *Shelburne Essays VIII*, More compares scientific naturalism to sentimental and emotional naturalism, and then embarks on long tangential discussions to show the relation between those evils and all phases of society; in fact, he gets around to just about everything except Huxley. He half apologizes at the end for the intellectual formulas he employs and pays his respects to the true beauties of romanticism. Ordinarily, however, More does not range so wide and free. He is often content with a brief aside on some modern evil. In his article on Gray in *Shelburne Essays X*, for one example, he concludes with this praise of the poet's moral restraint:

> Certainly to us, who live in a time of incontinent extremes, the very balance of his mind may be a source of quiet delight, in which we come to love the man . . . for his pensive philosophy.[4]

More often devotes whole essays strictly to problems of style and literary genre. His essay on Thomas Hood, for instance, is a study of the technique of poetic wit, punning, metaphor, and conceit with quoted illustrations and comments. Another example might be his remarks on the development of *vers de société,* or his very fine study of *Paradise Lost,* in which he argues that the poem is in the pastoral tradition because the real theme is the loss of the "pastoral ideal," the earthly paradise.

We noticed earlier how More wants the critic to applaud as well as censure, and on many occasions he abides by the principle. When he writes of Chesterfield, for instance, he mentions briefly that the author's morality is indeed faulty but that this has been over emphasized. He seems anxious to dwell on Chesterfield's better nature. At times, however, this saccharin

94

strain in More's criticism becomes almost too sweet and critically worthless, as in the discussion of an obscure American writer, Donald G. Mitchell. That essay is a literary travelogue with irrelevant anecdotes and pretty pictures, and it ends with the cliché, "Now as we take leave of our poet . . . ."

In a study of Arthur Symons in the first book of the *Shelburne Essays,* More dsplays what are probably the most typical qualities of his criticism. His method is to announce his ethical principles, illustrate them, and then apply them to Symons's poems. In this case he makes an analysis of the ideas in the verse rather than an open attack on socialists and humanitarians. It is also typical that the whole basis of his judgment of Symons is that the poet suffers from an inordinate desire for sensual delight, a "terrible disillusion of the flesh," which can only end in submission to ever coarser appetites and the spiritual death of complete indifference to moral responsibility.

So much for Paul Elmer More's practical criticism. Like Babbitt, he is a man of vast knowledge and considerable sensitivity, and he devoted his life to literature; yet his work is far short of great. Why this failure?

My answer is, first, that the doctrinaire Neo-Humanists, Babbitt and More, are limited in much the same way that a doctrinaire Communist critic is. While Marxist theories can throw light on a work, on an artist, or on his time, still a rigid Marxist can use them like a sledge hammer to flatten anything that will not fit his understanding of the party line. He may, for instance, apply his evolutionary standards to *all* kinds of literature; he may constantly demand a picture of an (inner) class struggle in society; he may see the hated Fascism everywhere he looks; and he may insist on explicit revolutionary action in every work.

The trouble is that the doctrinaire Marxist is more interested in a new society than in anything else. If he thinks that the literature will contribute to that goal, then he overrates it. But if the literature does not lead directly to that end, then he underestimates it. And the more impatient he is about the social goal, the more he will demand that art contribute to it.

In so far as the Marxist or the Neo-Humanist fits this form, he is really an enemy of the critical intellect. The point is that the Neo-Humanist's principles may help one understand and evaluate a work, but Babbitt and More often use them to lash an author who does not toe their party line. And Babbitt is undoubtedly the more serious offender. He castigates humanitarians, romantics, and naturalists of all kinds; he refuses to accept the influence of either heredity or environment on an individual; and he always demands his limited version of the inner struggle. The trouble is obvious. Babbitt is a radical reformer, of a kind, who insists that literature serve his cause.

The difference between the two leading humanists, moreover, is one of degree, not kind, but the difference is still significant. In general, More aims at literary estimates; he is willing to qualify his judgments; he is less apt to leap to the social evils to enforce his argument. Also, More demonstrates his subtlety by trying to deal with all the features of a work, even though a mistrust of analysis precludes the close application and development of some of his most interesting theories. It may also be true that he is more interested in the art because he is less interested in reform. When he forgets his violent prejudices, when he does not mechanically apply dualism or the principle of control, then he writes persuasively. There are occasions when he does just this, and one of the best is the study of Hawthorne. That particular essay is an analysis of the intellectual influences on the artist. He sees Hawthorne as a man cut off from the old religious faith of his ancestors, and yet still plagued by a belief in the depravity of man. He clarifies Hawthorne's conception of evil and especially the artist's idea that one must seek retribution through solitude.

This sort of history of ideas analysis is excellent, but when the moral critic becomes so doctrinaire that he aims doggedly and dogmatically at reform he will probably by-pass the art. He may claim broad principles, but they narrow in use.

This is an obvious risk in the ethical approach. And yet there is an even greater risk if one withdraws from the world. As Benedetto Croce puts it:

> Those intellectuals who see salvation in the withdrawal of the artist or the thinker from the world around him, in his deliberate non-participation in vulgar practical contests—vulgar in so far as they are practical—do without knowing it compass the death of the intellect. In a paradisal state without work or struggle in which there are no obstacles to overcome, there can be no thought, because every motive for thought has disappeared; neither any real contemplation, because active and poetic contemplation contains in itself a world of practical struggles and of affections.[5]

What we want, then, is an ethical critic who deals explicitly with the art, but whose ideas will by implication still apply to the general life. Yvor Winters comes closer to meeting this standard than either of the Neo-Humanists. He is as much concerned with the moral value of literature as they are, but in a new and different way.

CHAPTER V

Yvor Winters

Students of literary criticism often claim that Yvor Winters is some sort of latter-day Neo-Humanist who continues Babbitt's work. William Barrett, for example, says in an article in *The Kenyon Review:*

> Winters is very much under the sway of Babbitt—I think more even then he acknowledges—but it is doubtful that he has carried his morality very much further than Babbitt (with whom it was largely a matter of tone and attitude, prejudice rather than principle) toward some final basis.[1]

Or in *The Armed Vision*, Stanley Edgar Hyman claims that Winters' word "moral" is perhaps an equivalent for the humanist's "inner check." And Hyman observes, "For his moral emphasis, the core of his critical position, Winters seems chiefly indebted to the Neo-Humanists, particularly to Irving Babbitt."

To be sure, there is some reason to link Winters and Babbitt. For one thing, they both feel that the moral evaluation of literature is central to the critic's work, and they both object to many aspects of romanticism. More than this, Winters himself has considerable respect for Babbitt. He admires the fact that Babbitt defended literary criticism as an academic discipline and attacked the colleges for neglecting it. In the preface to *Primitivism and Decadence* he calls Babbitt one of "the few great critics of recent years" and, at another point, he says of Babbitt, "I admire him, and have learned a good deal from him."

But the too close association of Winters and Babbitt is unfortunate, because it confuses the history of American letters and encourages a misunderstanding of Winters's point of view. If anyone tries to read Babbitt's favorite "dualism" or "higher will" into Winters's work, he will just make a hopeless mess of Winters's theory. This sort of confusion, I think, is what occasions Hyman's complaint that Winters's use of the term "moral" is "complicated," "contradictory," "inconsistent," or "simply meaningless," because none of these adjectives is appropriate unless one tries to force Winters into Babbitt's mould.

Actually Winters himself has pointed to many of the important differences between his work and that of Babbitt. For instance, Winters writes in firm defense of reason, and he objects that Babbitt does not admit the "primacy of reason," that Babbitt's "higher will" is beyond reason. When Babbitt gives us a supra-rational emotional experience as a guide for conduct, Winters says, we have a philosophy that is "little better than a starting point for a short cut back to Emersonian mysticism." In the final analysis, then, Babbitt has "no explicit ethics of positive action," and his inner check is little more than a way of feeling.

And when Winters turns to Babbitt's treatment of literature, he finds that the older man's work has "tremendous errors and limitations." Babbitt is "obviously imperceptive in writing about poetry," and so often "misunderstood fine poems" that he ended by saying "stupid things about great" works. But his most sweeping objection to Babbitt's criticism is that it is "gravely vitiated by an almost complete ignorance of the manner in which the moral intelligence actually gets into poetry." Actually, if Winters is similar to any of the humanists, he is closer to Paul Elmer More than he is to the others; and in his contribution to *The Critique of Humanism* he calls More the best critic of the group.

99

The key concept in Winters's criticism is not control, but balance. Man's chief end, morally, is to exercise judgment so he can maintain a balance between his understanding of experience and his emotional response to that experience. Preserving one's balance is "sanity" and "in its own nature a good," and failing to preserve one's balance is "madness" and "in its own nature and quite obviously an evil." A madman, for instance, has such a blurred understanding of experience that his feelings, which are motivated by his illusions, are sure to be out of proportion. Indeed, his feelings may be so intense that there is a sharp maladjustment of emotion to understanding. And the failure in perception which occasions the imbalance signifies a lack of moral intelligence. If this sort of maladjustment can occur, then it is also possible to achieve an appropriate balance between feelings and perception, and the man with the greatest moral intelligence is the one who can exercise judgment in the face of any experience to maintain a proper understanding and the feeling appropriate to it.

But we can not exercise judgment in a vacuum. Our decisions must be guided by ethical theories and by practical experience with those theories. An adequate moral theory is any one which enables us to understand our feelings, to evaluate events correctly, and to comprehend the nature of sin. Winters thinks that St. Thomas Aquinas probably composed "the most thorough and defensible moral and philosophical system . . . that the world has known," but *any* "morality which preserves one from this loss of balance is defensible beyond argument by virtue simply of the fact that it so preserves one; and a morality . . . is evil, simply by virtue of the fact that it aims at loss of balance."

Here then is an ethical critic who does not insist on any par-

ticular ethical principles, and an ethical critic who also understands that "a treatise on poetry stops with the consideration
of the speculative judgment" as it appears in literature. He is
constantly concerned with the moral quality of the art rather
than general ethical problems.

But the moral problem for the writer is similar to the problem that all men face. If life presents us with the necessity of
understanding our experience and affecting a proper balance
between our perception and our feelings, then the poet also
faces that problem *as an artist* and *in his art*. In short, the poem
itself displays the quality of his moral intelligence. In fact,
the poem offers a unique opportunity for a more delicate and
precise refinement of perception and feeling than one ordinarily has. The poet's understanding and emotion at the time of
the actual experience may be "provisional and confused" compared to what he can achieve later on when he has a chance to
clarify and modify his feelings and to make the "judgment
possible in the poem." Of course, the paraphrasable content is
a significant sign of the poet's understanding, but Winters insists that "the paraphrasable content of the work is never equal
to the work, and . . . our theory of literature must account not
only for the paraphrasable content, but for the work itself."
What this actually means is that any detail of rhyme, meter,
or word has moral significance, and must be evaluated as it
contributes to the moral quality of the whole.

Here again the key idea is balance: the balance between the
rational statement and the feeling in the words; the balance
between the motive and the emotion. The terms Winters
uses may change with the context, and the particular meaning
may change slightly with the context too. For instance, the
balance in a poem may be that of idea to feeling, or meaning
to feeling, structure to emotion, logical content to emotion, the

rational structure to the rhythm, or the meaning to the convention. When he speaks of the novel, the terms may refer to a balance of significance to tone, or of a character's action to his feeling. The same concept of balance may also apply to an artist: Emerson's understanding may be weak, but his feelings intense. It may apply to a whole tradition: Puritanism contains an illogical and contradictory ethical doctrine, but it can arouse intense moral feelings in the faithful. Finally, the basic notion of balance may apply to individual words, and here the relation is one of the conceptual meaning of the word to its connotations, or its denotation to its connotation. Whatever the terms—and this list simply illustrates some of the possibilities—they all derive their meaning ultimately from the notion of balance. The feeling of a poem, for example, is seen "mainly by way of the non-paraphrasable content," and the relationship is that of cadence, rhythm, and the connotations of words to the rational content of the work. The "value of the poem resides precisely in the relationship between these two elements," and any successful detail will communicate the feeling proper to its subject. The rational statement may govern the possibilities of feeling which can be derived from it, but the poet tries to adjust feeling to motive precisely. He has "to select words containing not only the right relationships within themselves, but the right relationships to each other." And Winters warns us that we do not have a simple relation of understanding to emotion, but "once the process begins we have a complex interplay of the two, each enriching the other." In Winters's view, then, the artist's work is "evaluating and shaping (i.e., controlling) a given experience," and trying, in that manner, "to perfect a moral attitude toward that range of experience of which he is aware."

Winters's notion that the rhythm of a poem may be morally significant is unusual enough so that it occasions considerable misunderstanding, and one example of this appears in his essay on John Crowe Ransom.

> In *Primitivism and Decadence,* where the whole problem of meter is discussed more fully than I can hope to discuss it here, I wrote:
>> . . . in traditional verse, each variation, no matter how slight, is exactly perceptible, and as a result can be given exact meaning as an act of moral perception . . .
> and Ransom, in quoting this passage, adds the parenthetical comment, "though he means merely the exact phonetic value." The fact of the matter is that I meant what I said.[2]

While one can understand why Ransom tries to translate Winters's statement, still it is evident that Winters *does* mean what he says. In his critical system, rhythmic variation *is* morally significant, and we must turn to his principles of meter to see just why this is so.

The meter of verse, Winters says, is the arithmetic norm of the line, the regular pattern; and the rhythm, on the other hand, is the controlled departure from the norm, the variations on the regular pattern. Together, the meter and the variations help to establish the feeling of the work, and they allow the artist to express more powerful feeling and finer shades of feeling in poetry than one finds in prose. Of course, Winters agrees that the meter of an unknown foreign language is not very effective, but when the meter exists simultaneously with all the other elements in a known language, then it can stimulate the emotion appropriate to the meaning. The meter of *Paradise Lost,* for one instance, contributes successfully to the feeling. The blank verse "functions as an instrument for the expression of something essential to the poem." In this fashion, different metrical forms may express different kinds of feeling and "great complexity of feeling." The poet does not invent a logical argument and then put it into verse, for he is endeavoring to bring each word as close to a true judgment as possible. As Winters explains:

> It is for this reason that I have spoken of meter as having moral significance . . . . The total phonetic value of metrical language has the power to qualify the expression of feeling through language. Since the expression of feeling is a part of the moral judgment as I have defined it, the meter has moral significance, for it renders possible a refinement in the adjustment of feeling to motive which would not otherwise be possible.[3]

He sees meter, therefore, as an opportunity for the exercise of judgment, and he prefers a metric pattern so clear that the slightest variation may be apparent. He asks that the "full sound-value of every syllable" be willed for a "particular end" and that it be "precise in the attainment of that end." His main objection to free verse is that the norm of heavily accented syllables is so slight that there "is no exact basis for judging" any metrical variation, and very little chance for subtle or slight divergence. When experimental "meter loses the rational frame which alone gives its variations the precision of true perception," then it has abandoned a powerful poetic device which more traditional verse employs; for in traditional verse the metrical pattern is clear, and "each variation, no matter how slight, is exactly perceptible, and as a result can be given exact meaning as an act of moral perception." Of all the traditional verse forms the couplet is the most flexible, because it has "an obvious substructure . . . over which poetic variations may move, from which they derive exact identity," and "it can suggest by discreet imitation, the effects of nearly any technique conceivable."

Thus, Winters may employ the idea of balance to analyze meter and, indeed, any aspect of a work. In *Primitivism and*

Decadence, for instance, he gives us an elaborate set of techniques for detecting a lack of balance in literature. Although he is mostly concerned with poetry, still many of the concepts can by analogy apply to any literary form, and many of the illustrations are from other *genres.* His whole emphasis there is on the obscurity which results when the rational content of a work is so reduced that the feeling is weak or false, and the relationship between the two is disproportionate. When poetry eludes paraphrase, then the "poet's sensibility to the connotation of language overbalances his awareness of the importance of denotation" and his work suffers from obscurity. The "seven types of pseudo-reference," for example, are practices which reduce the rational coherence of literature at the same time that they create an illusion of rational coherence. If a poet like Robinson Jeffers, for example, employs the structural method of simple repetition in a purely narrative work, then the poem can have little narrative unity or progression. Or romantic irony, for one other illustration, is a corruption of feeling in the poet, a feeling which he cannot approve or control, and which ultimately "entails a corruption of style—that is, an admission of careless feeling."

Winters's distinction between the "primitive" and "decadent" poets illustrates still another use of the idea of balance. The decadent poet has a fine sensitivity to language and a wide range of experience, but his "work is incomplete formally (in the manner of the pseudo-referent and qualitative poets) " or his work is "weakened by a vice of feeling (in the manner of the better post-romantic ironists) ." The primitive poet, on the other hand, suffers no particular difficulty in achieving total form, but his range of experience is limited.

In other words, the primitive enjoys an easy victory. Of course, any successful poem makes some demand on the artist's moral judgment. Even in a purely descriptive work, the poet must still evaluate the experience for what it is worth, for even simple "description renders the feeling appropriate to purely sensory experience and is hence a kind of judgment of that experience." But that poem "will be most valuable, which, granted it achieves formal perfection, represents the most difficult victory," and the greatest tragic poets, such as Shakespeare, achieve a victory over life itself. As he says:

> Shakespeare wrote the plays in order to evaluate the actions truly; and our admiration is for the truth of the evaluations . . . . And how, one may wonder, can Shakespeare evaluate these actions truly except from the position of a moralist? To evaluate a particular sin, one must understand the nature of sin; and to fix in language the feeling, detailed and total, appropriate to the action portrayed, one must have a profound understanding not only of language, for language cannot be understood without reference to that which it represents, not only of the characters depicted, but of one's own feelings as well; and such understanding will not be cultivated very far without a real grasp of theoretic morality.[4]

As this statement about Shakespeare indicates, Winters is just as concerned about the relation between literature and conduct as Babbitt is, for the two would agree that literature is a potent force for good or ill. As Winters sees it, the whole question of the power of poetry is quite complex, but it is obvious that a poem may simply and literally possess us. That is its true magic. Thus, the reader can, through great literature, increase his awareness of experience. And that new knowledge may render "greater the possibility of intelligence in the course of future action." In fact, "the great poets . . . offer us . . . the finest understanding of human experience to which we have access" and through them human intelligence is "kept alive." And if the best literature displays the finest moral judgments, then it can train our power of judgment and should affect the moral quality of our daily lives.

But it is also true that poetry can be a potent force for evil. If the poet sets up "false ideals of human nature" and judges "experience in terms of them and so beguiles us into doing likewise, the human intelligence is to that extent diminished." Winters is, of course, not professionally interested in censorship, only evaluation, but he warns us of the presence of evil. He would say, for instance, that we are in considerable danger if we enter the mind of Hart Crane, Whitman, or Emerson "with our emotional faculties activated and our reason in abeyance." But once we understand the evil in these men, Crane, for instance, then we may profit from their virtues with impunity. Even all the experimental and decadent poetry may "be valuable as a point of departure" if one is aware of its deficiencies. But some writers have such great and evil genius that they endanger "the literature of our time."

If poetry can have such a profound influence, then the critic's task is pretty well cut out for him. In general, the critic must evaluate the moral quality of the art, but he should approach the goal with five important steps. First, the critic should record any historical or biographical data necessary to understand the mind and the method of the author; second, he should analyze the literary theories that are relevant to the work; third, he must make a critique of the paraphrasable content; and fourth, he must make a critique of the feelings motivated by the experience; and, last of all, he must judge the work. And if the poem itself is a moral judgment, then the critic has to understand and evaluate it as such. If a good poet needs moral intelligence, then a good critic needs the same sort of intelligence, because his judgment is no less a moral exercise than the creative act itself.

The critic's judgment, however, "cannot be communicated

precisely," because "no critical term can possibly be more than a very general indication of the nature of a perception." With much more verbal sophistication than the early humanists ever show, Winters realizes that literary judgments reflect one's feelings. As he puts it:

> . . . when one speaks of standards of critical judgment, one does not ordinarily think of weights and measures. One has in mind certain feelings of rightness and completeness, which have been formed in some measure, refined in a large measure, through a study of the masters. The terms that one will use as a critic will stand for those feelings.[5]

Winters's notion of the critic's function will be complete if we look finally at the kind of criticism he repudiates. As we have seen, he disavows didactic criticism which attends only to the paraphrasable content and so fails to account for the work itself. He also attacks the romantic and hedonistic critic of the Walter Pater variety who pursues emotion, elusive and meaningless nuances of feeling, and often ends in "disillusionment with art and life." He opposes any attempt to separate art and action, because the divorce tends to make the art an esoteric indulgence separated from other human affairs. And finally, he believes that the romantic critic is right to take account of the "power which literature seems to exert over human nature," but that he is wrong to emphasize only the "emotional experience" of the art.

The Practice

We come now to Winters as a practicing critic to see just how he employs some of these theories in specific literary judgments, and we will examine, in turn, his treatment of poems, novels, and philosophical prose.

While Winters shares with Babbitt and More a deep suspicion of many modern literary tendencies, still he differs greatly in one respect: he has devoted "the central study" of his life to the work of such recent writers as Gerard Manley Hopkins, Robert Bridges, T. Sturge Moore, Allen Tate, Howard Baker, Edwin Arlington Robinson, Robert Frost, T. S. Eliot, Agnes Lee, William Butler Yeats, Wallace Stevens, William Carlos Williams, Marianne Moore, Mina Loy, Hart Crane, Ezra Pound, R. P. Blackmur, and John Crowe Ransom. As Winters tells us, "Their problems have been my problems; their success or failure has been the focus of my experience." When he talks about scanning free verse, he laments that few readers will follow the discussion because a full understanding requires a

> . . . thorough knowledge of all the best poems employing the medium in the second and third decades of our century, a sensitive and conscientious study of several years in duration, the immersion of the student in a particular way of feeling, the acquisition of a new and difficult set of habits of hearing and of audible reading.[6]

And in truth, his analysis of versification does show comprehensive study, intellectual virtuosity, and uncommon sensitivity to poetic form. This is hardly surprising, for Winters is himself a remarkable poet. While his poetic ability does not necessarily improve his stature as a critic, still it does add authority to his comments. For instance, he refers to personal letters from Crane and Williams, or he illustrates his scansion of free verse with one of his own poems. When he says, therefore, that the problems of modern poets have been his own, we can take the words quite literally. He is one of them and one of the best.

Winters describes his first book of criticism, *Primitivism and Decadence* as "mainly a discussion of style," and it is an extended discussion of techniques employed by writers who suffer from an imbalance of perception and feeling. Since none of the other books has such an elaborate analysis of style, this one can serve as a basic reference because it contains detailed definitions of terms that he sometimes refers to in later criticism. But the great variety of theories and evaluations brings on a difficulty. Sometimes the remarks are left in almost outline form. There is, for one example, a thumbnail essay on Robinson Jeffers which contains a description of the poet's philosophy, a criticism of those beliefs, and an evaluation of seven of the longer poems—all in about three pages. It is so condensed that it is almost over before you realize what has happened. If the essay were expanded, it might be more persuasive. As it stands, it is a pronouncement.

All the later books, however, are essentially different from the first. *Maule's Curse, The Anatomy of Nonsense,* and the *Function of Criticism* are collections of extended treatments of individual writers. There are a few essays on such literary subjects as the modern critic, or "the reading of poetry," but, in the main, he focuses squarely on particular artists, and most of them Americans. In most of these essays he is also concerned with the intellectual forces that influence the author and the art. As he explains:

> The relationship of the history of ideas to the history of literary forms (or) the intellectual and moral significance of literary forms, has not been adequately studied: yet this subject is the very core of literary criticism and of the understanding of the history of literature.[7]

In his study of ideas, moreover, Winters is especially attracted to the effects of the romantic movement, for here is, "essentially, a rebellion against the authority of reason in favor of the authority of impulse and emotion." Of course, Winters defends reason and warns against certain aspects of romantic philosophy. For instance, he objects when the romantic accepts a "pantheistic philosophy or religion." According to this type of romanticism, self-expression is good, and literature is a perfect form for self-expression. There is nothing in this theory, he feels, to enable the artist to avoid a kind of automatism, for "Romantic doctrine itself will not restrain him." Its influence has been dominant for some time now, and he declares, has been "obviously disastrous in literature." In his essay on Robert Frost, he finds, for example, that the principles of Greek and Christian thought tend to save the poet's talent, but that the principles which

> . . . have hampered Frost's development, the principles of Emersonian and Thoreauistic Romanticism, are the principles which he has openly espoused, and they are widespread in our culture. Until we understand these last and the dangers inherent in them and so abandon them in favor of better, we are unlikely to produce many poets greater than Frost, although a few poets may have intelligence enough to work clear of such influence; and we are likely to deteriorate more or less rapidly both as individuals and as a nation.[8]

Romanticism in Winters's view has several different forms, and it influences literature in various ways, not always harmful; but, in general, romantic ideas encourage the artist into the deadly sin of obscurity. A poem is obscure when it has little or no rational frame, or when it displays feelings which are not clearly motivated by the rational content. He insists on a rational content, because he feels that without it no work can succeed. Moreover, the rational content roughly sets the limits of the feeling. Any kind of obscurity is evidence of a lack of moral intelligence, because a balanced mind capable of accurate judgment has a clear understanding, and feelings in proportion to the perception. All the features of his criticism, then, the causes and effects of obscurity, the effects of romantic ideas and

111

of traditional ethics—all of these are directly related to his fundamental ethical axiom. While the terms are not always moral ones, they can appear at any point, because the entire discourse rests on a moral frame.

And, as his remarks on Frost suggest, Emerson plays a major role in Winters's account of the influences at work in American letters. I think it is not misleading to suggest that Emerson is for Winters what Rousseau is for Babbitt. In Winters's eyes, Emerson is the personification of evil, the romantic pantheist and a potent force. To illustrate Winters's estimate of Emerson, we will look first at his comparison of the unknown Jones Very with Emerson, second at Winters's study of Edwin Arlington Robinson, and finally at his essay on Hart Crane.

In Winters's comparison of Very and Emerson, neither writer comes off very well, but what is important for our purposes is that Very's poetry and philosophy are held to be superior to Emerson's. Very surrenders to a Christian God, who, fortunately, disapproves of one's surrender to emotions. Very's God also serves him by supplying traditional Christian moral standards. In contrast to this ethical firmness, Emerson simply cultivates feelings. Since Emerson believes that all impulses are of divine origin, his philosophy eliminates the possibility of rational choice and a theory of value which can serve as a basis for rational action.

Jones Very, who exists "in a state resembling madness from a strictly moralistic point of view," is, moreover, a practicing mystic. He denies the real world. And Very's truth is absolute, but it is obtained by mystical insight and revelation. It should be clear that this kind of irrational pursuit of truth is so sharply different from Winters's own procedure that he regards Very as a luxury for those ordinary souls who live in the real world of common sense. Naturally enough, Winters admits that Very's mysticism makes the core of his poems obscure, but even so, by

112

implication and by analogy many of the poems give us a picture of normal, comprehensive human experience. And in some of them, the explicit Calvinistic doctrine is so abstract that it can be taken as merely a general comment on the value of humility and endurance.

With Emerson, on the other hand, we have a philosopher who makes all truth relative. Emerson talks mysticism, but he is not even a real mystic. In short, Winters says, Jones Very is superior to Emerson both as philosopher and as poet.

Much the same picture of Emerson appears in Winters's study of Edwin Arlington Robinson. In this case, however, the subject is Emerson's influence on Robinson. When Emerson teaches that emotion and instinct are the "voice of God," he gives irresponsible romanticism a pseudo-religious tone; he lends moral sanction to mere eccentricity, to self-satisfaction, and to critical laziness. For this reason, Winters argues, anyone who follows his first guesses in matters of opinion and perception and has only irritated contempt for argument, anyone who believes that careful thinking is somehow beneath him, is Emerson's true heir. Robinson is that heir, apparently, for the poet inherited just that kind of intellectual laziness. Needless to say, the Emersonian doctrine in Robinson runs counter to his best work.

Although the Emersonian influence does not ruin Robinson's style, it does result in "loose thinking and in a good many failures of structure." Winters calls attention especially to certain defects which run through Robinson's longer poems. For one thing, Robinson withholds information about the subject under discussion so that one never understands the nature of the important emotions which are being analyzed. Often, Robinson has "nothing in particular in his own mind," and this sort of intellectual indolence even makes for weakness of characterization. Both these faults Winters traces to Robinson's weakened sense of relevance which, in turn, results from a moral curiosity that is insufficiently guided by ethical principles. In each case, moreover, the failure occasions unnecessary confusion and obscurity in the art.

Winters asserts, however, that the poet also falls heir to another trait which tends to strengthen his poetry. A strong moral sense, inherited from the New England moralistic tradition, dominates the work. As a result, Robinson displays a curiosity about moral problems in his subjects and an admirable honesty and clarity in his style. Robinson's characters, like the author himself, show a tenacity of purpose and an ability to "sustain themselves in loneliness on some kind of inner integrity." The shorter poems particularly reflect a subtle and penetrating application of the spiritual values of the Christian tradition. The poem *Hillcrest*, for example, is an explicit negation of the Emersonian tradition, for it acknowledges the tragedy of life and the value of contemplation; and it expresses neither despair not triumph, but rather a calm evaluation of the world.

Thus, the Emersonian influence weakens Robinson's poetry, but it does not ruin it. Winters believes, however, that Hart Crane completely accepts Emerson's philosophy as he discovers it in Whitman and that the ideas have truly disastrous effects on both his life and his work. According to Winters, Crane actually lives Emerson's dictum that the "unreflective creature of impulse is the ideal; he is one with God and will achieve the good life and good art." This philosophy encourages Crane to cultivate alcoholism and homosexuality *on principle*, and it leads him ultimately to madness and suicide. The effect on his poetry is just as fatal. Crane gives free reign to his emotions and mystical impressions and pays little attention to meaning. As a result, Winters insists, his poetry eludes paraphrase. Crane's sensitivity to the connotations of words so

114

overbalances his awareness of the importance of denotations that his work is, in the main, loosely constructed and incomprehensible. The style is carelessly, even purposely obscure. Despite the fact that Winters finds a few passages which rank with the best romantic poetry, Crane is so seduced by his romantic attitudes that he revels in violent feelings which have no clear motive.

Somewhat paralleling the fatal effect of Emerson's influence on Crane is Ezra Pound's influence on modern poetic technique. This note occurs all through Winters's criticism, but especially in the study of T. S. Eliot. He ends that piece with the suggestion that Pound's influence on modern prose and verse is as widespread as it is destructive. He says:

> . . . and when one seeks closely to find the features of the divinity, the primal spirit of the age to whose will surrender is required, one may well be appalled; for behind the shadows thrown by veil after veil of indeterminate prose one will find, if one is patient, the face of Ezra Pound in apotheosis.[9]

And I mention Pound's role here not to dwell on it, but only to point out that Emerson is only one evil influence in modern poetry.

There is probably no better illustration of Winters's emphasis on the intellect than his insistence that an author's understanding of the ethical issues be proportional to his moral sensitivity. When an artist's moral sense is great, and yet not supported by a clear understanding of ethical principles, the unbalance occasions obscurity in the writing. In Winters's opinion, Henry Adams, Hawthorne, and Melville all illustrate the point. While these men have considerable sensitivity to ethical problems, their grasp of theory is so weak that their work suffers.

This important critical principle plays a large part in his

analysis and evaluation of Henry James. The considerable moral sense in James is "a product which subsisted as a traditional [Christian] way of feeling and of acting after the ideas which had formed it, and which . . . had long supported it, had ceased to be understood, or as ideas, valued." New England Calvinism, for example, helped to intensify his moral sense, for even after Calvinistic theology died out, the strong moral sense lived on, an emotional cultural lag. James's moral sense was further stimulated by the fact that he lived in Europe, for his feelings of inadequancy about American culture made him all the more sensitive to moral issues.

But James's heightened moral sense was not accompanied by a firm enough ethical perception. His moral sense was weakened, for instance, because it was cut off from its religious source by the influence of ill-digested scientific truths and by the corrupt influence of romantic philosophy. And, in addition, James was deeply affected by the crude code of America's "Robber Barons." All of these together so weakened his ethical understanding and his ability to believe, that his great moral sense existed precariously.

Yet, urged on by his heightened interest in ethics, James actually built his plots out of moral choices, but his characters exist in a kind of moral vacuum, because they have no realistic limitation on their choices. His people are so divorced from ordinary customs that they are often little more than allegorical personages rather than particular people. And James's characters have the same sort of precarious moral sense that plagues the author. They read into situations much more than seems justified. They concentrate intensely on trivia. In that fashion they build up their moral pressure to great heights, but we seldom learn just what causes these emotions, so the action remains obscure. Thus, the characters themselves are uncertain, and James cannot judge the uncertainty. Curiously enough, however, Winters feels that this ethical uncertainty does not mar James's best work. In several novels, he acknowledges, the plot is completely sound, but he devotes very little space to these compared to the attention he gives to obscurity.

In an essay on Henry Adams, for one more example, Winters goes back to the middle ages to trace the intellectual forces which affect Adams. This is a problem similar to one which we found in James, because the Adams of the *Education* has a strong moral sense, an earnest desire to read ethical meaning into the universe, and yet he has so lost his faith and his will to believe that he can not justify his own life. In other words, Adams's feelings run high, but his understanding is nil. And the cause of his difficulty is rooted in the acceptance of faith over reason. According to Winters, St. Thomas Aquinas wisely separated faith and reason, but William of Ockham tended to blur the distinction by giving new power and position to faith. This rise of faith, Winters says, made possible an irrational doctrine like Calvinism. The logical contradiction of upholding *both* determinism and free will is endurable, he asserts, only if it is supported by a strong Calvinist faith. But when reason finally weakened the old theology and Calvinism lost its hold on the faithful, the old support for ethics also disappeared. Although a gentlemanly Unitarianism grew up where Calvinism once held sway, it could not take the place of the older faith nor supply Adams with a firm enough religious conviction for his excited moral sense; so that Adams, like Henry James, was left with intense moral felings but without faith or real understanding.

The Adams essay is a good example of what Winters means by historical background, but in his essay on Poe he does not try to uncover the historical forces at work on the artist, nor even to place Poe historically. His method here is to move directly to Poe's critical theories and to expose what he calls the shoddy and excited sentimentalism of the work. He charges that Poe tries deliberately for strange, fantastic, hidden meanings—in other words, that Poe tries to be obscure; creating a wilful dislocation of feeling from understanding. At best, it is merely "art to delight the soul of a servant girl."

We have seen something of Winters's view of the American Puritans, but his interest in the Puritan influence is so important a part of his criticism that we should examine it more closely. In his study of Hawthorne, for instance, Winters argues that the artist's New England heritage not only encourages the allergorical technique, it is also clearly responsible for his artistic failure. In Winters's eyes, the Puritan distinction between the damned and the elect is a "long step toward the allegorization of experience, for a very broad abstraction is substituted for the patient study of the minutiae of moral behavior long encouraged by Catholic tradition." The individual's behavior becomes a symbol of his position among the chosen few or among the damned, so that any sin is evidence of damnation, and any sin, Hester Prynne's for instance, easily comes to represent all sin. Hawthorne unconsciously accepts this disposion to allegorize and creates in *The Scarlet Letter* a work "faultless in scheme and in detail," one of the "chief masterpieces of English prose." He intensified "pure exposition to a quality comparable in its way to that of great poetry." While the characters have a few individual qualities, a few simple human traits, still they are precise representations of abstract ideas.

However, the contradiction between predestination and a belief in moral responsibility leads eventually to the fall of Puritanism. In the name of God the Puritans cut themselves off from human nature. As Winters explains it, Hawthorne is rational enough to be critical of the Puritan morality, but he has no adequate doctrine to take its place. Had Hawthorne been able to analyze and organize ideas as well as he

118

dramatized them in *The Scarlet Letter,* he might easily have overcome the difficulties. When he turns his back on the simplified conceptions of his Puritan ancestors, however, he abandons "the only orderly concepts, whatever their limitations, to which he had access, and in his last work he is restless and dissatisfied." In *The Blithedale Romance* and the unfinished romances, according to Winters, Hawthorne has all the mannerisms of an allegorist—all the machinery—but there is no clear meaning for the symbols. Unable to write realistic fiction, then, Hawthorne eventually is unable to write even allegory. Cut off from any consistent and organized ethical views, Hawthorne's understanding becomes blurred, his writing obscure.

This study of Hawthorne raises an important problem which is a natural consequence of Winters's literary theories. It may be stated in the form of a question; if the causes of Hawthorne's literary ambiguity in the unfinished romances can be explained, how does it happen that the same writer could earlier produce a masterpiece like *The Scarlet Letter?* The more Winters builds up the case for Hawthorne's later failure, the more we must ask that he account for Hawthorne's early success. We have seen that in the James essay, Winters devotes his attention entirely to the historical causes of obscurity and brushes past the question of James's faultless novels with a sentence or two. In that case we may excuse the haste, because his explicit aim is to deal with only certain elements in a few works, but in the Hawthorne essays he tries to display the writer's virtues as well as his faults, and he does not satisfactorily bridge the gap between the two. Of course, Winters does remind us on many occasions that the balance which the American artist achieves, at any one time, exists precariously, but the point is that Winters does such a good job of establishing the precariousness of the balance that one finds it difficult to understand how the artist ever achieved it or, if he did, to understand why he later fell so precipitously into meaningless obscurantism. This difficulty in Winters's criticism appears in many of the studies, but it comes out most clearly in his remarks on Henry Adams. In the first part of that essay, Winters explains carefully how Adams was destroyed morally and intellectually by his failure to achieve any justification for his life, his work, or his writing. Adams's philosophy, Winters tells us, nullified Adams's choice, judgment, and comprehension—and only weakened moral feeling persisted. When we come to a third section of this essay, however, we discover that a few years earlier Adams wrote the famous *History of the United States During the Administrations of Thomas Jefferson and James Madison* and that the Adams of the *History* has full possession of his faculties. His delineation of character is faultless: honest and perceptive. The style is expert and flexible. In fact, Winters claims that the *History* is clear evidence of a precise intelligence. He compares Adams with Hume, Gibbon, Macaulay, Prescott, Motley, and Parkman, and ranks him unequivocally with the best English or American historians.

Now Winters could claim that there is a difference between the moral perception necessary to write a history and that required for an autobiography, but he draws no such distinction. Lest there be any doubt of this, we should examine his exact statement. He says:

> The relationship of literary quality to historical scholarship in a work of this kind perhaps needs to be briefly considered. The historian such as Gibbon or Macaulay, one is inclined to suppose, examines his material to the best of his ability, and on the basis of that examination forms a fairly definite idea of the characters and actions involved. In this stage of his work, he is comparable to the novelist who has long meditated his characters and outlined the plot. The final literary form of the history

represents an evaluation, a moral judgment, of the material which he has held in his mind. Such judgment is inevitable, even though the historian refrain completely from any didacticism: it resides in the very act of writing, and no historian, be he a good stylist or a bad, can escape it.[10]

How is the Adams of the *History* capable of the irresponsible and wilful obscurantism of his later years? Winters says that the death of Adams's wife will not account for the change, and that Adams's difficulty with his publishers will not give us a satisfactory explanation. With these ruled out, he concludes, "Probably it was merely the accumulation of emotion, the result of an ancestral tendency, which finally reached a state where it influenced his action definitively." This statement, whatever it means, falls short of being an adequate explanation of how, in a relatively short space of time, Adams could possess the highest level of moral perception, and then soon after lose it so completely.

The same problem appears in Winters's study of Melville, for the author's powers of moral navigation are so great when he writes *Moby Dick* that it is "one of the most carefully and successfully constructed of all the major works of literature," and the form and subject are mastered with a success equal to that achieved by Milton, Virgil, or Shakespeare; yet Melville is in a "moral limbo" when he writes *Pierre* and *The Confidence Man*. Even the prose of these books is excited and inflated. Here again Winters says that Melville's grasp of ethical principles was never sure, but it was sure and strong enough to write *Moby Dick*. It may be that Winters feels that the explanation of Melville's decline and fall is beyond his range, that it is a problem for the psychologist, not the critic. However, the question does rise out of his literary and ethical theories, and his explanation is not always adequate.

In Winters's study of Wallace Stevens we find not only a more satisfactory solution of this difficulty, we also encounter a good example of another significant aspect of his criticism: his mistrust of hedonism. The Stevens poem *Sunday Morning* is, in Winters's opinion, one of the best poems of our time. With a careful analysis of the work, he demonstrates that the language is firm in structure and sensitive in detail.

In this poem, however, Winters discovers hedonistic ideas and attitudes which, he believes, slowly debased the greatest poetic talent of the twentieth century, and he tries to show how they are related to the poetic faults. *Sunday Morning* is an expression of the love of emotion, for the question in the poem is, what is divine about the woman, and the answer is that her emotions are divine—that emotions are good in themselves. But the more Stevens follows this philosophy in his career, the more he seeks intense feelings divorced from understanding, and he suffers eventually the ennui which results from such a hopeless pursuit. In later poems the mild ennui of *Sunday Morning* becomes contempt for his art and romantic self-parody. Instead of renouncing his art, however, Stevens adopts a "sly look and a perverse ingenuity in confusing the statement of essentially simple themes." Winters contends that Stevens purposely tries for obscurity with the vain hope that "some note more moving than the poet has a right to expect may be struck from the obscurity." In the early years, Winters concludes, Stevens was able to maintain a "dangerous but successful balance," but the traditional element finally gives way to a hedonism which ultimately weakens the verse.

This high regard for Stevens's *Sunday Morning* is significant, because it brings us to the delicate question of the value of a poem which has a philosophy quite contrary to his own. As we have seen, both Babbitt and More tended to judge literature by the degree to which it mirrored their own views. That is not the case with Winters. He argues that one need not hold the poet's views in order to enjoy the work—and his high regard for *Sunday Morning* is an illustration of the principle at work. Even though the poem is discreetly didactic and teaches a dangerous philosophy, still he admires it greatly because, as he explains, hedonists do exist, and *Sunday Morning* is an accurate and beautiful expression of the point of view. "It is no more necessary that one be a hedonist in order to enjoy this particular poem than that one be a murderer in order to enjoy *Macbeth*." While it is true that the poem offers us only a small portion of experience, and mistakes that part for the whole, it is nevertheless a successful description of that portion.

And Winters carries the point about the truth of the poem further. He says, for instance, that we may rule out some poems which contradict elementary facts of experience, but others we can retain. Some of Blake's poems, if read as Blake intended, offer us a nonsense view of experience, but those same poems are stated so abstractly that one can simply take them as advising us to do good and avoid evil. Thus, in some poems, Winters admits, we may have to give the poem "as much of our own private meaning as the nature of the statement permits," no matter what the artist intended. As we have seen, it is for this reason that Winters admires the mystical poetry of Jones Very, because by analogy his poems can be taken as comments on the real world. In the case of religious poetry, Winters holds that the true believer may share more of the experience than the non-believer, but at the same time he says that religious poems can mean something to the non-Christian. Of Dante's *Divina Commedia*, he says:

> The non-Christian, however, might easily share a wide community of belief with Dante. The portraits of the damned are portraits of human beings, represented in Hell as they might be seen in life, suffering for sins most of which are acknowledged to be sins by intelligent men, whether Christian or not. As we proceed, however, toward

123

the final vision of beatitude, we find ourselves dealing with concepts which are more and more purely Christian, and it is more than likely that only the convinced Christian can feel the poetry at something like its full value: for the rest of us, the poetry offers theoretic projection of the imagination, a representation more or less dramatic. Not purely, however: for such poetry will of necessity be colored by feelings, desires, and ideas common to all men, and this alloy renders easier our entrance into the Christian state of feeling.[11]

Perhaps his remarks on a poem by Allen Tate will help to gather together many of these points about his criticism and will illustrate them, too, because his comments show how he looks beyond the paraphrasable content to find evidence of the moral equilibrium of the artist. Here, first, is the short poem by Tate, and then we will look at Winters's evaluation:

The Subway

Dark accurate plunger down the successive knell
Of arch on arch, where ogives burst a red
Reverberance of hail upon the dead
Thunder, like an exploding crucible!
Harshly articulate, musical steel shell
Of angry worship, hurled religiously
Upon your business of humility
Into the iron forestries of hell!

Till broken in the shift of quieter
Dense altitudes tangential of your steel,
I am become geometries—and glut
Expansions like a blind astronomer
Dazed, while the worldless heavens bulge and reel
In the cold revery of an idiot.

Winters points out that a prose paraphrase of the poem would have to record that the author is saying that "as a result of his ideas and of his metropolitan environment, he is going mad." But, that is simply not the whole poem, for it leaves out the non-paraphrasable element of "feeling." Once we look at the whole poem, we discover that the sonnet "indicates that the author has faced and defined the possibility of madness . . . and has arrived at a moral attitude toward it, an attitude which is at once defined and communicated by the poem." The feeling of the poem, then, is really one of "dignity and of self control in the face of a situation of major difficulty, a difficulty which the poet fully apprehends." He observes finally that any attempt to eliminate the rational content would confuse the feeling, for the worth of the work consists in the simultaneous "relationship between the two."

CHAPTER VI

The Epilogue

This last chapter is designed to do double duty. It will have to serve as a conclusion and, at the same time, an epilogue. With the rather detailed chapters on the three critics behind us, we can compare their work in the larger sense, looking for similarities and differences which now stand out; and the comparison will give us the opportunity to make some additional points about Yvor Winters.

First, then, let us look at a significant difference between Winters and the two Neo-Humanists. Both Babbitt and More talk about "decorum," and, as they use the term, they mean mediation between two extremes. They ask us to exercise "control" so that we can hold a balance between the two. But a "religious dualism" so dominates their thinking that "control" means not so much balance (or indeed anything like mediation) as it does that we should vigorously surpress the evil side of our nature. In other words, they would have us struggle to overcome the evil that is within; and, if we are to win the battle, we need more than ordinary human power. We need the active help of the supernatural, for Babbitt the higher will and for More the Supreme Being.

In contrast, Winters's idea is that we must maintain a balance not between inherently opposing forces, but between various aspects of the personality. He says that we must struggle to achieve a state of equilibrium, and the point of the effort is not to suppress the evil in us, but to maintain the balance. Our desire for sensation, for example, is not an evil in itself. When it is divorced from understanding, however, it is undesirable, and the loss of balance is the evil.

And, according to Winters, we must also work to bring our ideas into correspondence with reality. Thus, with all our knowledge, our values, and all our intellectual skills, we confront a complex of forces, and we live the good life if we can maintain the equilibrium that is ordinarily called sanity. There is, moreover, no supernatural power to help us achieve the balance. Religious beliefs may help, religious faith may help, religious habits may help, but we are ultimately left alone with only ordinary human powers and the problem of adjustment.

Thus, while Babbitt and More hold to an older religious dualism, Winters has a view of man that is post-Freudian. I do not mean that Winters uses Freud's terms or precisely Freud's hypotheses, but I do mean that, like Freud, he takes the central problem to be that of maintaining a mature balance of interrelated aspects. And he follows Freud, too, in thinking that an individual's balance is rather precarious, subject to change. As we have seen with Melville and Hawthorne, writers may achieve the state at one time, and lose it the next.

This idea of balance is a central theme, appearing often in his poetry as well as his criticism, and the poem *Sir Gawaine and the Green Knight* is an especially effective statement of the concept. In a prose comment on that work Winters explains that the Green Knight represents sensation

> trying a human, the human surviving more through habitual balance than through perfect control at the height of the temptation, but gradually recovering himself. If you like, at a more general level, it is the relationship of the artist toward sensibility: Crane was a Gawaine who succumbed. This theme, if reduced to its most general

terms, is the theme of most of my best poems for the past seven or eight years, and the explanation of it is easily to be found in my criticism.[1]

As the poem itself shows, Gawaine's moral conviction and ingrained habits save him:

Reptilian green the wrinkled throat,
Green as a bough of yew the beard;
He bent his head, and so I smote;
Then for a thought my vision cleared.

The head dropped clean; he rose and walked;
He fixed his fingers in the hair;
The head was unabashed and talked;
I understood what I must dare.

His flesh, cut down, arose and grew.
He bade me wait the season's round,
And then, when he had strength anew,
To meet him on his native ground.

The year declined; and in his keep
I passed in joy a thriving yule;
And whether waking or in sleep,
I lived in riot like a fool.

He beat the woods to bring me meat.
His lady, like a forest vine,
Grew in my arms; the growth was sweet;
And yet what thoughtless force was mine!

By practice and conviction formed,
With ancient stubbornness ingrained,
Although her body clung and swarmed,
My own identity remained.

Her beauty, lithe, unholy, pure,
Took shapes that I had never known;
And had I once been insecure,
Had grafted laurel in my bone.

128

And then since I had kept the trust,
Had loved the lady, yet was true,
The knight withheld his giant thrust
And let me go with what I knew.

I left the green bark and the shade,
Where growth was rapid, thick, and still;
I found a road that men had made
And rested on a drying hill.[2]

Another important point about these critics is that all three
of them, and especially Babbitt and Winters, take the history
of ideas approach to literature. But Babbitt is so anxious about
conduct generally that art becomes incidental to the main task
of showing how the ideas affect society. Winters, on the other
hand, is interested in how the ideas affect the artist's balance,
and the evidence of that is in the art. Paul Elmer More certainly tries to deal with the relation between the artist and the
work, and he holds theories which encourage this, but he stops
short. It is at this very point that Winters has an advantage
over the Neo-Humanists because he began his work at a time
when it was becoming fashionable to analyze the poem in order
to find the relation of all the parts. While this intense focus
on the structure and texture of the work, as some critics call
it, is not new in criticism, it has been in vogue during Winters's
tenure as a practicing critic. In fact, analysis has been so
popular that some have left the larger problems of history in
order to concentrate on single works. In his own fashion,
Winters reflects this feature of modern criticism, and his power
of exegesis is as great as any. Even in the eyes of a rather
unfriendly observer, Winters is

> impressive as a close and imaginative reader, and several
> critical readings in the book [*Maule's Curse*], particularly
> a detailed analysis of the allegorical symbolism in the scene
> from *The Scarlet Letter* where Hester and Pearl wait in

129

Governor Bellingham's mansion and see themselves distorted in a mirror, are quite penetrating.[3]

But all the analysis in Winters's criticism is in the service of his moral theory, because it is designed to show the state of balance in the work. And his remarks on *Moby Dick* will illustrate this fact. He sees that novel as essentially a problem of moral navigation. The sea is "obscure," the "unknown," the area of "instinct," "feeling," "danger," "terror"; while the land is the "known," the "mastered in human experience." In order to test his power of judgment, man must venture out into the sea without losing his position with respect to the land. Man can live successfully only by means of perception so trained in abstraction that he can find his way amid the shifting and chaotic phenomena of the half-known. The problem in *Moby Dick,* therefore, is basically that of moral judgment. It is the problem of the relation between principle and perception. Ahab destroys his nautical instruments, the compass and so on, which give him his position; he tries to sail by instinct, and will not listen to the warnings of Starbuck, who represents the critical intelligence. When Starbuck finally submits to Ahab, then madness wins out, and sanity and morality are destroyed. The tragic end of the novel is the inevitable conclusion of Ahab's insane refusal to heed Starbuck.

Winters's power of analysis also makes him an effective enemy of obscurity in modern verse. As R. P. Blackmur says:

> No critic has done more to deflate, in detail, specifically, under your nose and your mouth, the final value of poetry, however otherwise valuable, which fails to declare its subject.[4]

And the same intellectual agility he shows in analysis precludes the prejudiced and automatic reaction to certain kinds of subject matter that we saw in Babbitt and More. The practical effects of this difference are great, and we can illustrate by comparing Winters's attitude toward Baudelaire with More's and Babbitt's. The subject matter of Baudelaire's poems alone was enough to make both humanists shudder and turn away. Winters, however, is so subtly sensitive to the treatment of the subject, and to the author's attitude toward it, that the subject itself is not necessarily an indication of the moral worth. In fact, Winters believes that Baudelaire achieves "the most remarkable balance of powers in French literature after Racine." Baudelaire consistently and accurately evaluates his experience. The subject matter of his poems is "no more evil than the materials of Shakespeare . . . for both explore human nature rather far; both depict evil, and make us know it as evil." Even in a poem like *Une Martyre,* which deals with a sadistic murder, the poet treats the subject for what it is worth, richly and fully, and so displays the highest degree of moral intelligence.

This brings us to another point about these critics, and it is that all of them take the evaluation of literature quite seriously. They all agree that the real purpose of literary scholarship and criticism is to help us judge the art. It may be that they are, as a group, too critical, even censorious, in their dislike of romantic literature, for example, but at least they never dodge the final responsibility of judgment. And in their different ways they are also keenly aware that the critic must persuade his audience. This is not the time for a rhetorical analysis of their work, but all three are experts in the art, and Babbitt may be the best. It is exciting to follow a formidable figure like Babbitt, one who believes so deeply and sincerely, and one who tries so hard to convert his audience. This fact may help to explain why Babbitt was such a successful teacher and why his *Rousseau and Romanticism* has been reissued in a popular paperback.

Although his rhetorical style is radically different from the

131

other two, Winters also has a marvelously persuasive, vigorous, and logical mind. And whatever else one may say about his critical theory, it does seem to fit him. Writing *is* for him a moral judgment, and this makes him all the more impressive.

But their skill in rhetoric also encourages these critics into a one-sidedness. For example, Babbitt is the prosecuting attorney when he deals with Rousseau. He is not trying to give us *the other side,* because he feels that he must present the case against the defendent. Of course, Babbitt keeps reminding us of what he is up to, but it is possible that Babbitt's case against Rousseau might be even more effective if he were not quite so intent on the unattractive features of the Frenchman.

For my own part I have trouble with Winters on this same score, and his treatment of Poe is a case in point. I would agree that Poe is a childish thinker, almost out of his class when he tries his hand at serious criticism. And Poe's poems and stories, too, are certainly not great art; so Winters's case is sound enough. But he carries the attack too far. Poe's work is youthful perhaps, but an effective and skillful kind of art that will probably last, because it is among the best of its kind. And the "kind" is not unimportant.

I have the same sort of objection to the picture of Emerson that one gets from Winters. Here again I could not argue that what Winters says about Emerson is untrue, but only that it is not "all about" Emerson. There are many other aspects to that many-sided New Englander, but one can not find them in Winters's work.

I am especially uncomfortable when Winters talks so freely about Emerson's influence. For example, it is difficult to see just how Emerson is responsible for Robinson's intellectual laziness. What sort of influence is it? Personal? Direct? Indirect? The troubles abound, but they all come from the fact that a literary argument which attempts to show the influence of one mind on another should proceed with the greatest caution, because one must eliminate all other causes of the condition before he can establish a particular relationship.

In addition to this one-sidedness, there is another feature of Winters's work which is not persuasive. I refer to what has been called the "flat *obiter dicta*" in his books, and I find this an unattractive curiosity. Winters likes to record just how he ranks poems in much the same way one might report the order of finish of an important race, so that a work, for instance, may be called "the finest contemplative poem of the last twenty years." On one occasion he simply lists seventeen of the "best" poets of our generation, and one or two of their "finest" poems. This is perhaps the logic of evaluation carried to a kind of absurdity; but it should be clear that this sort of flat judgment is rare. In the main, Winters's evaluations are bolstered by carefully persuasive arguments and evidence.

One final point about this critical trio. They have all played a useful part in helping to bring criticism into the graduate schools as an important branch of literary learning. Babbitt was one of the early voices raised against the idea that literary scholarship in America should be modeled on the "objective" and "scientific" work of the German graduate schools. Babbitt himself was *The Professor*. He knew almost everything everyone else did, and he used it all to evaluate. He was *The Professor Critic,* and he was also so learned that he helped to make criticism acceptable.

The American version of the German scholar in Babbitt's early days did dominate the graduate schools. He worshiped the doctorate and demanded what he called "facts." He was uncomfortable about evaluation and tried to avoid it. Curiously enough, as Babbitt and others pointed out, this work was as evaluative as any criticism, but the judgments were implicit and largely unsupported. In fact, the philosophy of the worst of that old fashioned scholarship was much like that of a movie fan club. *Any information* about the "stars" was cherished. But Babbitt, More, and others began to ask questions about "greatness." Who were the literary stars? And they insisted that the scholars themselves should face the fundamental question of the value of the art.

By now the battle to get criticism into the schools is largely over. Winters is one of the many critics who teach and write the business of the evaluation of literature is now considered central to the study of the art, and it is generally agreed that evaluation is never finished. Changes in our understanding, our knowledge, and our needs will mean that we must constantly reexamine and reevaluate our literature—old and new. And professional and non-professional students need all the help they can get from the finest critics. Winters, for one, seems to me wonderfully helpful in judging modern poetry. He is no representative of a fading genteel tradition, yet he finds much modern work morally imperfect. And the direction of his effort seems fruitful. In the moral measure of literature he has gone further than anyone has before, but Paul Elmer More also clearly understood the fundamental postulate of this approach. As he put it:

> The fact is that ethics and aesthetics are inseparable in art. Or, more precisely, just in proportion as the practice or criticism of art becomes superficial, ethics and aesthetics tend to fall apart, whereas just in proportion as such practice or criticism strikes deeper, ethics and aesthetics are more and more implicated one in the other until they lose their distinction in a common root.[5]

Notes

CHAPTER I

[1] Herbert J. Muller, *Science and Criticism* (New Haven, 1943), pp. 261-262.

[2] James T. Farrell, *A Note On Literary Criticism* (New York, 1936), pp. 176-177.

CHAPTER II

[1] Plato, *The Works of Plato* (New York, N. D.), translated by Jowett, p. 397.

[2] Samuel Johnson, *Lives of the English Poets* (New York, 1929), pp. 62-63.

[3] Joseph Wood Krutch, *Samuel Johnson* (New York, 1944), p. 493.

[4] Samuel Johnson, *op. cit.*, p. 84.

[5] *Ibid*, p. 108.

[6] Joseph Wood Krutch, *op. cit.*, p. 316.

[7] William Hazlitt, *The Collected Works of William Hazlitt* (London, 1902), ed. by Waller and Clover, Vol. V, p. 1.

[8] *Ibid.*, p. 65.

[9] Matthew Arnold, *Arnold's Essay on Wordsworth* (Boston, 1925), ed. Benjamin R. Ward, p. 139.

[10] *Ibid.*, p. 140.

[11] Oscar Wilde, *Complete Works of Oscar Wilde* (Boston, 1909), ed. Robert Ross, Vol. IV, p. 183.

[12] *Ibid.*, p. 19.

[13] Walter H. Pater, *The Renaissance* (London, 1910), p. 239.

[14] Walter H. Pater, *Appreciations* (London, 1922), p. 38.

[15] James Russell Lowell, "The Function of the Poet," *The Century,* XLVII (1894), pp. 432-439.

[16] James Russell Lowell, *American Critical Essays* (London, 1940), ed. Norman Foerster, p. 77.

[17] *Ibid.*, p. 82.

[18] Edgar Allan Poe, *The Complete Works* (New York, 1902), ed. J. A. Harrison, Vol. XIV, pp. 271-272.

[19] *Ibid.*, pp. 197-198.

CHAPTER III

[1] Irving Babbitt, *Rousseau and Romanticism* (New York, 1919), p. 367..

[2] Irving Babbitt, *Democracy and Leadership* (New York, 1924), pp. 6-8.

[3] Irving Babbitt, *Rousseau and Romanticism,* p. 287.

CHAPTER IV

[1] Sherlock B. Gass, *The Criers of the Shop* (New York, 1930), p. 230.

[2] Paul Elmer More, *New Shelburne Essays* (Princeton, 1936), Vol. III, pp. 80-81.

[3] Paul Elmer More, *Shelburne Essays* (Boston, 1917), Vol. X, pp. 19-20.

[4] *Ibid,* p. 276.

[5] Benedetto Croce, *The Age of Analysis* (New York, 1957), ed. by Morton White, p. 49.

CHAPTER V

[1] William Barrett, "Temptations of St. Yvor," *The Kenyon Review,* IX (1947), p. 535.

[2] Yvor Winters, *In Defense of Reason* (New York, 1947), pp. 551-552.

[3] *Ibid.*, p. 551.

[4] *Ibid.*, p. 561.

[5] *Ibid.*, p. 76.

[6] *Ibid.*, p. 104.

[7] *Ibid.*, p. 155.

[8] Yvor Winters, *The Function of Criticism* (Denver, 1947), p. 187.

[9] Yvor Winters, *In Defense of Reason,* p. 501.

[10] *Ibid.*, p. 415.
[11] *Ibid.*, p. 476.

CHAPTER VI

[1] Yvor Winters, "Sir Gawaine and the Green Knight," *The New Republic,* LXXXXI (1937), p. 104.
[2] Yvor Winters, *Collected Poems* (Denver, 1952), p. 113.
[3] Stanley Edgar Hyman, *The Armed Vision* (New York, 1948), p. 58.
[4] R. P. Blackmur, "A Note on Yvor Winters," *Poetry: A Magazine of Verse,* LVII (1940), pp. 146-147.
[5] Paul Elmer More, *New Shelburne Essays* I (Princeton, 1928), pp. 108-109.